SEX
COMES
FIRST

SEX COMES FIRST

 **15** ways to save your relationship

...without leaving your bedroom

JOEL D. BLOCK, PhD &
KIMBERLY DAWN NEUMANN

Avon, Massachusetts

Published by
Adams Media, a division of F+W Media, Inc.
57 Littlefield Street, Avon, MA 02322. U.S.A.
www.adamsmedia.com

ISBN 10: 1-59869-971-7
ISBN 13: 978-1-59869-971-5

Printed in the United States of America.

J I H G F E D C B A

Library of Congress Cataloging-in-Publication Data
is available from the publisher.

This publication is designed to provide accurate and authoritative information with
regard to the subject matter covered. It is sold with the understanding that the publisher is not engaged in rendering legal, accounting, or other professional advice. If
legal advice or other expert assistance is required, the services of a competent professional person should be sought.
　　—From a *Declaration of Principles* jointly adopted by a Committee of the
American Bar Association and a Committee of Publishers and Associations

Many of the designations used by manufacturers and sellers to distinguish their product
are claimed as trademarks. Where those designations appear in this book and Adams
Media was aware of a trademark claim, the designations have been printed with initial
capital letters.

This book is available at quantity discounts for bulk purchases.
For information, please call 1-800-289-0963.

CONTENTS

INTRODUCTION

C opulation and coupledom. Coupledom and copulation. When it comes to a fulfilling relationship, these two, sex and coupling, are intrinsically linked. In many cases, the correlation is positive (happy couples frequently report healthy sex lives), but sometimes, it can be a double whammy. Why? Because the road to being a dynamic duo, for both men and women, is mined with potential issues that can taint romance. For example, lack of communication, unresolved anger, and mistrust are the kinds of problems that may result in a sex life that is mediocre at best and more likely distinctly unfulfilling.

What it comes down to is that couples with relationship concerns don't feel erotically connected. Maybe they have intercourse once a week, but complain the "spark" is missing. Maybe they haven't made love in a month, several months, a year, or longer, in which case sexual awkwardness can be added to the problems that keep them apart. Whatever the case, there is no doubt that relationship issues affect what is going on between the sheets as well.

Typically, couples will go into therapy and work on their conflicts with the hidden hope that one day they will get along better and their romantic life will jump-start. And often this works. Passion is reignited. But it is usually a lengthy process.

These couples are looking to improve their situation by enacting the typical "Feel something, and then do something" action plan. Not surprising when you consider that's probably the approach most of us take when facing a challenge in our lives. We're socialized to follow an isolate-the-problem/find-a-solution scenario. Trust us, there's nothing wrong with more romance following better communication and relationship harmony. In fact, if that's the outcome, fantastic!

But there's another approach that will add enormous power to a couple's relationship and strengthen as well as hasten the gains made by talking things out. It's characterized by "Do something to feel something." And, it involves sex.

Now, don't get too excited. We're not suggesting that you stop trying to communicate and just get busy. It's not that easy. However, sexualizing your issue with a specific physical encounter that is consistent with your issue *after* working on it verbally can markedly enhance your chances of resolution, because there is a visceral/muscle memory component that is closely linked to your emotional state. In short, integrating a "mind" solution with a "body" solution creates synergy and results in a powerful mind/body experience.

We are suggesting that instead of leaving a problem discussion and letting the words exchanged fade, it will be more effective to reinforce those words with an experience that will literally get into your skin. In other words, involve your body in the process, and your mind will follow.

The sexual experiences throughout the book are powerful. Consequently, fears, doubts, anxieties, shyness, and other apprehensions are likely to get triggered initially. These feelings are common but transient; once the experience proceeds the emotions will likely become strongly and positively bonding.

Of the many forms of couple intimacy—a smile across the room, a kiss, a touch—sex has the potential to be the most powerful positive physical experience most of us enjoy. This is especially true if sex results in emotional fulfillment, better communication, security, reassurance, and intimacy—and that's precisely the aim of this book. We want to teach you to capitalize on the power of sex not only to help enhance physical intimacy with your partner, but also to help connect you in ways that allow your conjoined emotional life to stay on solid footing.

An important thing to keep in mind is that negative feelings thrive in secrecy and lack of acceptance. Integrating couple issues through positive experiences that feature skin-to-skin contact is the precise antidote for healing negative feelings. How so? Well, when you venture into these experiences, you will be sharing while in a state of naked vulnerability, literally. The result is that as you lose your clothes you will simultaneously be forced to strip away additional emotional layers that might be hindering your issue resolution. It's more difficult to ignore or deny difficult feelings when your proverbial armor is removed. This means that your shared experiences while in a state of undress may be ramped up well beyond traditional interaction.

Sex Comes First is the first book to combine the traditional talk approach to strengthening couple relationships with sexuality. Not only will we discuss the most common couple issues—those that bug almost all of us and sap the erotic energy right out of our relationships—but we'll also help you learn how to use sexual interaction as a means of issue resolution right now (instead of waiting until it's "fixed" to return your sex life to red-hot status).

Yes, you read that correctly. The right sexual act at the right time can actually help resolve many of your issues as a couple . . . today.

Think of yourself as an adventurous scientist who is interested in adding some punch to the usual way of approaching relational issues. The experiments you will be doing will help integrate the more traditional emotional tools that strengthen relationships in a physiological way. Or more simply put, the body is a powerful tool and involving your entire being in your relationship will get you further than ignoring the mind/body connection. And as an added bonus, your sack sessions will get more interesting at the same time.

Get ready to take your sex life where it's never been before. Your relationship will thank you.

Chapter

ANGER GETS IN THE WAY

The dramatic slammed door exit. The thrown glass. The infamous face slap. The exasperated flood of tears. Chances are you know the classic signs of an angry outburst. Unless you're part of a couple for whom that kind of volatile back-and-forth serves as foreplay, anger probably gets in the way of your sex life.

No doubt almost every couple will experience flare-ups in response to the sporadic squabble. However, little tiffs and even a fiery shouting match now and then can be helpful if it brings the real issues into the light for resolution. In other words, occasional arguments don't lead to long-term sexual turnoffs. In fact, you've probably even had angry sex before, but the more likely result of anger in a relationship is that it simmers someplace down below the surface waiting to find a sneakier way to manifest than an outright verbal explosion.

The bottom line is that anger is a complex emotion and straight-up angry sex where that raw feeling is present and recognizable only happens on occasion. More frequently, anger ends up masked as something else. That's when things get tricky because subterranean anger is the deadliest kind, not only for your relationship but also for your sex life.

With that in mind, the first step to dealing with anger in your relations with your partner is learning to differentiate between the different types of anger. That involves recognizing that some-times anger may look quite different than, "Frankly my dear, I don't give a damn."

Straightforward Versus Stealth Anger

When it comes to anger, there are two types: the straightforward and the stealthly. Figuring out which kind you're dealing with can really help you try to work through a meltdown in your rela-tionship with your mate. So, how do you know the difference?

Straightforward Anger

Think about this: What makes you boil? What evokes anger to the point that you can't contain yourself and all your feelings come tumbling out? Do you have that visual? That is probably the perfect example of visible anger. Usually when anger reaches that kind of a tangible state, the issue is likely on the table and ready for resolution.

In many ways, the kind of anger that you see and recog-nize is easier to handle than other types. Why? Well, when you actually know what is causing dissension between you and your partner, then there is a marked improvement in the probability that you'll be able to find your way to the core of the issue and move forward (for better or for worse). In other words, volatility may promote velocity when it comes to anger resolution. However, that only holds true if the reason for the anger is authentic and not an exasperated attempt to deal with another issue lurking beneath the angry surface.

Stealth Anger

The other kind of anger is the silent and deadly stealth anger that can absolutely undermine a couple's emotional and sexual connection. The reason this emotion gets so complicated has more to do with these hidden huff-makers than the obvious outbursts. With that in mind, let's look a little closer at each of these types of anger.

Unvoiced Anger

With this type of hidden anger, the problem stems from the fact that one or both partners in the relationship are harboring resentment but do not bring it to the other's attention. It's the everyday equivalent of you saying, "What's wrong?" and your partner answering, "Nothing." You still have a nagging feeling that something isn't kosher with you two. Or the opposite, your partner will start to sense that something is off-kilter in your relationship and will keep prodding you for affirmation of her suspicion.

But instead of just speaking up, you put on that happy face you've learned to wear and say, "Everything is fine." The problem with the word *fine* is that when someone uses it, things usually are not fine. Think about it. When things are fabulous between you two, do you use the word *fine* to describe your state of affairs?

Not likely. But if things are strained and you're not speaking up, the word *fine* pops out of your mouth.

The problem with unvoiced anger is that it can be sensed. So, one partner will keep asking and the other will keep denying, while getting more and more annoyed that his partner just can't figure it out. Remember this: Except for a very few possibly psychically gifted individuals, most people aren't mind readers. If you don't speak up and say what you're thinking, your partner may never figure it out. Remember that little thing called communication? Like it or not, you pretty much have to have it if you want your relationship to survive.

The other problem with unvoiced anger is that it tends to grow over time. It is a mistake to not bring up the issue for serious discussion. Avoiding issues that are troublesome is anything but benign. If not worked out, even if it is difficult, resentment will build up and create a major obstacle to openness. After some time of this behavior, the underlying anger gets between the couple in small increments that eventually become insurmountable. It is as if she is adding another brick to the wall between them each time until the wall is impenetrable.

When you or your partner finally voice frustration, it may come tumbling out in decibels way beyond typical human vocal production.

Unrecognized Anger

Sometimes, the maelstrom brewing inside you is so craftily concealed even you aren't able to recognize it as anger, which adds another layer to unspoken anger. Accordingly, not only do you keep your feelings from your partner in this scenario, you keep them from yourself through denial or minimizing (e.g.,

"I'm not angry, I'm just annoyed."). Another example would be that oftentimes what couples call "boredom" is actually code for a long-harbored hidden resentment. The key word here is *hidden*. All too often, individuals don't recognize that the root of the emotion they're feeling towards their partner stems from fury.

Many times people are taught to suppress anger. In so doing, with practice they get very good at shifting their emotions or learning to classify what they're feeling as something else entirely. This may seem like a prudent way of dealing with extreme emotions like anger. The only problem is that when you are mad about something and can't figure out that the emotion you're feeling is anger, it will continue to fester. Eventually, like with unspoken anger, it will have to reach a level that is above boiling point before it is recognized, and by then, the damage may be insurmountable. This is especially true if the ramifications of unrecognized anger start to spill over into other areas (e.g., everyday life and in bed), and the relationship starts to suffer on many fronts as a result of this hidden emotion.

Unrecognized anger will brew—that is guaranteed—until it is recognized. It's extremely persistent, so don't think you can outwit it just by fooling yourself into thinking you're happy when you're not. It will all come out eventually—be prepared.

Unresolved Anger

Negative feelings do not simply evaporate if left unattended; they tend to swell and permeate the relationship, sapping positive energy that could be directed toward romance. We know you're thinking: *Well, duh, if I'm mad of course it's going to permeate the relationship.* It's really not that simple, however. In this scenario, anger may have come up and there might even have been a fight. So, you'd think that this was no longer in the "hidden" category. However, if you walk away from a fight still feeling deeply hurt, uneasy with the resolution that was discussed, or even without a solution to the issue, then the feelings are still unresolved and the anger attached to this issue will resurface.

It's not enough just to get mad and move on. There has to be some sort of progress towards resolving the anger (and the issue) or there will be a rebound effect. How so? Well, there may be a slight respite in the feelings once the issue has come to the surface, but as soon as either party has had some time to reflect, she will likely realize she is still angry. But there will be a hesitancy to revisit the issue with her partner because things will probably already be a bit tenuous and unless the couple has thrown in the proverbial towel, they will likely be trying to rebuild from their disagreement. Unfortunately, it's difficult to recover relationship equanimity when one or both partners are still holding on to some tension.

See how this becomes a deadly cycle? When the anger is not resolved, it will continue to loop around until the issue is finally addressed in a way that allows the couple to break the cycle and move forward. Until that fateful day, however, this type of hidden anger is bound to repeat itself.

Issue-Confused Anger

Frequently a couple may find themselves having a major argument over something that's not really the issue at the crux of their anger. In this case, the real issue causing the anger is the *hidden* part. You might also call this "Sneaky Anger."

What would be an example of this? Well, consider the couple that is really having issues about finances. Perhaps they are trying to save to get a bigger apartment but the woman can't seem to stop buying pricey new outfits for work, or the guy is spending a lot of money playing in several fantasy football leagues. Over time, these little shopping or play habits may start to really bother the other partner especially if he is curbing spending habits in order to try and make the mutually set goal of getting a bigger domain in which to live. But, instead of addressing the issue about finances, the offended partner starts picking on his significant other about something inconsequential and unrelated such as how much time they spend on the computer in the morning checking e-mail. See the disconnect?

The problem with this kind of issue-confused anger is that the *real* issue doesn't get addressed and in the meantime, all these petty little complaints get added on top of it. The anger will not be effectively dealt with until you've then removed all the other issues to reveal the true problem. The result is a lot of confusion.

Retaliatory Anger

Another variation on the hidden anger theme, which may undermine a relationship, is when resentment has built up and it leads one partner to consciously or unconsciously retaliate against the other partner either by doing something that the other partner doesn't like, or by not doing something that is desired by the other partner. Usually, this leads to less cooperation and more hidden anger. In contrast, if the partner whose actions are retaliatory simply disagreed with the request instead of striking back (explaining the basis for that dissension), or offered an alternative solution—"I will get a job to support my extra spending," or "I will not use a housecleaning service, but I want to keep my gym membership"—there is basis for an open discussion. Even if one partner admits to going overboard—"I just couldn't resist those Jimmy Choos at that Sample Sale, it was a great buy and I have a weakness for killer pumps"—it would be better than insisting that there was full cooperation when clearly there wasn't.

While most inconsistencies between word and deed (or the manner in which a message is conveyed) may seem minor, they can have a powerful impact. If one partner tells the other, "You are the most important person in my life and my top priority," but in daily behavior is selfish, inconsiderate, and irritable, the message that is conveyed is something like this: "Your feelings and wishes are not as important to me as my own needs, and you can't really rely on what I say." The partner who is conveying the loving message but is not *being* loving is actually setting up a confusing situation for her significant other. When actions don't support words, over time it may lead an individual to feel underlying resentment without even realizing why.

Intimacy-Avoidance Anger

Fact: It's difficult to get closer to your partner if you're fighting all the time. As a result, many people who start to fear intimacy will find themselves starting intentional disagreements to feel safe.

Sometimes anger is also used intentionally to keep intimacy at bay. A signal that this is occurring is when things are going along well in the relationship, then suddenly one partner starts to pick fights over mundane things that previously had not caused any strife. However, when tension caused by a fear of intimacy is played out through anger, it is usually subconscious (i.e., intentional relationship sabotage stemming from anger is not the norm). Unfortunately, sexual indifference may also result.

Many couples genuinely want to be emotionally close to each other and share a passionate lovemaking partnership, but they reach a certain point and their fears take over. For example, one partner may start complaining about the other's socializing or one may actually go out too much after work, knowing full well that his partner will be put off. The issue splits them apart for a time, and then they become close again until they reach a point of closeness that one or the other is uncomfortable with and the pattern of sabotage repeats itself.

Consider the following statements. If you recognize these traits in your behavior, you might be using anger to avoid intimacy:

♂ I intentionally pick fights over silly things when I know I might be spending alone time with my partner.

♂ Instead of allowing myself to appear vulnerable in front of my partner, I always put on a strong "I don't care" front.

♀ When I have sex with my partner, I immediately jump out of bed afterward to avoid postcoital bonding.

With all of these covert combat creators, the important thing is to start to recognize them before they eat away at your foundation as a twosome. But once you begin to understand these anger termites, you can figure out how to more effectively deal with them before the blowup is irreparable.

Sex and Anger

No doubt anger, visible or hidden, will affect the quality of your sex life. Hidden anger will especially threaten to drive a wedge between you and your partner. The problem with these scenarios is that it can be difficult to recognize that the feelings affecting your sexual relationship are actually anger and not something else. We as humans are incredibly skilled at masking our emotions. So instead of looking at your partner and thinking "Wow, I'm so mad!"; you think "Wow, I'm not sure I want this person to touch me." Well, of course you're turned off! You're angry, hurt, or afraid. But you confuse the issue by assuming it's just sexual boredom, thus distancing yourself even further from the real problem at hand.

The first thing you need to do if you find yourself in a sexual ennui situation is to spend some time being honest with yourself. Think about your partnership and your partner. When was the last time you made love? Was it good? If not, when was the last time you had great sex? What happened between then and now? Is there anything you can think of that you might actually be angry about? Try to isolate the "what's-bugging-me" issue. If it's really sexual boredom, then a good sack session with one of you standing on your head or some other sexual variation should fix things up.

However, chances are there's something deeper going on. If you can successfully identify your hidden anger issue, it's smart to bring it up in conversation with your partner before moving on to the sexual reinforcement phase of this chapter. Why? Well to begin with, once you isolate the issue, sex is not going to be much fun if you're so mad at your partner you don't want her near you. But also, this is one of those situations where talking things out beforehand facilitates an even better physical connection. If you've already tackled the emotional part of this "fight," then returning to an intimate connection will be easier.

Confronting Anger Effectively

It's a choice. You can explode or you can be effective. Learning to confront anger in an adult, rational manner is a skill that you can learn. The trick is recognizing that you are feeling anger and then figuring out the best way to address the issue at hand.

As we've already laid out in this chapter, one of the most dynamic things you can do to deal with anger is to counter the tendency to duck it. Consequently, consider this: If your partner has accused you of being defensive, or if you realize that about yourself, make an effort not to block off the feelings hidden *behind* your usual reactions. Instead, reflect on the feelings that are lurking below. As you open to greater understanding of yourself, you will gradually begin to view your partner's emotional concerns as well as your own with more compassion.

Also consider taking the following steps when you realize you are face to face with an anger situation.

At First, Do Nothing!

Take a few moments to calm down before you respond. Uncensored anger in a love relationship is almost certain to be unproductive. It is a case of ineffective acting-out versus appropriate assertion. Raw anger is likely to be alienating, while considered anger may be difficult to receive, but connective. This is not to be confused with peace at any price; it is about having the maturity to express yourself in a manner that not only airs a grievance, but actually moves an issue to resolution rather than scarring the other person.

Recognize That Easily-Triggered Anger Is "Should"-Driven

Anger is triggered when we feel that someone or something is not behaving as we insist. What we don't realize is that the world rarely behaves as we think it "should." To avoid undue frustration and anger, it is wise to focus on desire—the desire for our partner to behave in a pleasing manner, and for circumstances to go our way—but not to insist that she has to. Desire thwarted leads to disappointment, insistence thwarted leads to rage. It is not about what should be; it is about avoiding making our preferences into demands.

Speak to Hurt Feelings

When we are let down, oftentimes we feel betrayed and hurt. For many of us, the hurt almost instantly converts into anger. This seems to be especially true for men. We've heard many women say, "My guy's cheap emotion is anger. He seems to feel nothing else, or if he does he never expresses it." Not expressing the hurt behind the anger is probably the most common relationship-discouraging behavior that occurs with couples. The partner on the receiving end is often defensive and doesn't hear the real issue, while the underlying issue survives to surface another day.

A better bet is to try to get what is bugging you out in the open as soon as possible. If your partner asks you if something is the matter, just tell him before it turns into full-blown hatred.

Focus on the Solution

To avoid misunderstandings, it is important to let others know what you want in specific terms ("What I really want is for you to be on time when we agree to meet at a certain time."). Don't expect others, even your mate, to read your mind.

Take Responsibility for Your Part in an Issue

There are very few issues leading to an outburst that are completely one-sided. Victim and villain, pure black and pure white is, with notable exceptions such as rape, simplistic. In relationships, there is a complexity that results in a shared responsibility for most issues that cause grief. The sharing may not be fifty-fifty, but it's rarely 100 percent on one side. Rather than simply pointing at your partner and blaming, consider your own part in an upsetting circumstance and be honest enough to bring it up. You will be increasing the likelihood that your partner will own her part in the issue and both of you will move more quickly to resolution.

If you can learn to confront anger effectively rather than just blowing up in the face of controversy, you will stand a better chance of learning to work together as a couple. Coinciding with the verbal part of this, however, is the physical. Anger raises your blood pressure, causes immune system stress, and can wreak havoc on the adrenals. In other words, when someone says he's so angry he could feel his blood boil, he actually might be feeling his blood heating up. The physiological responses to anger are intense. And sexually, anger may corrode a couple's intimate connection faster than acid. With that in mind, here are some ways to deal with the ramifications of anger in the bedroom.

Sexual Solution

Surrender (i.e., letting go) is an essential part of love and the antagonist of anger, which is holding on. There is, however, a lot of confusion about what *surrender* means. Some of us equate surrender with loss of personal power, which is not the case—that's submission. *Surrender* is used here to mean letting go and merging and making a conscious choice to open your heart to your partner, rather than standing back with alienating anger.

In the context of erotic, the word *surrender* is often used when the heroine allows herself to be swept away by the hero's passion. That's a very narrow view of erotic surrender. It limits the woman and leaves out the man entirely.

Think of erotic surrender as the act of letting go while aroused, not as ceding control to your partner. This is in the same way that letting go of anger isn't a loss, but rather a gain for your relationship. Most people enjoy the feeling of being in control of their lives, even though much of what happens to them is clearly beyond their control.

At first, surrender may seem counterintuitive, and it is. Successful people are admired not only for the money they earn and their accomplishments but also for the amount of control they exert over their environment and the others inside it. People who practice self-discipline are also admired.

In lovemaking, the man who can "control" his erection and ejaculation and the woman who can "control" her partner's arousal and her own responses are idealized. Where does surrender fit into this picture?

Surrender is an integral part of true intimacy. Letting go into full arousal is intrinsic to the higher level of sexual pleasures. It takes time to become comfortable with the process. Surrender is no easy matter. It's frightening to keep thinking, "I can't let go completely," but it makes sense to be frightened if you believe that you will lose yourself and not find your way back. The same applies with letting go of anger. There is the feeling of loss, but in reality it is an additive experience.

Letting go, whether it is in the bedroom or it is about letting go of anger, requires having a strong grip on yourself. It is about knowing who you are and being willing to reveal that and stand by it. In effect, it is a paradox: You will be able to let go when you have a good grip on yourself and who you are. Anger doesn't grow out of strength, but out of weakness. It is fear masked by aggression.

Surrender, whether to the erotic, or to toxic anger, is akin to climbing a mountain. If you feel in control of yourself, rather than directing your energy toward trying to control the elements, you can relax and take in the beauty of the climb. When you're tense and feeling out of control, the climb seems foreboding. Likewise, when you are tense and feeling out of control, you hold on to anger rather than releasing it.

The truth is that you cannot master the mountain; you master yourself in the process of climbing the mountain. Unfortunately, you can't wait until you feel perfectly safe and secure before you venture out for your first climb. Feeling safer comes as a result of the experience.

The bottom line comes down to this: You can reinforce the work you've done trying to let go of anger verbally by learning to let go physically. The following sexual suggestion is designed to help you practice surrender as an experience that will contribute to letting go, not only sexually, but of anger as well.

SEXUAL SLAVE

In this carnal experience you will learn to physically let go by turning yourself over to your partner. How so? Well, in order to reinforce the idea of releasing your emotions, try offering to be your partner's sexual slave for a night. Here's how:

Step 1

Tell your partner you are offering yourself to him in whatever capacity he or she desires (within reason, of course—if there is something that causes you pain or discomfort, you are welcome to set limits beforehand).

Step 2

Have your partner create a sexual script. That means, have her or him spell out exactly how the sexual encounter should go and what your partner would like you to do during the course of it.

Step 3

Be open to trying something new if your partner requests it. If you hate it, you don't have to do it again, but on the flip side, you may discover a new dimension to your sexuality this way. Keep in mind that by surrendering you may also feel threatened. Moving into areas that are new to you will likely result in an uncomfortable uncertainty, but if there is trust between partners and the sexual experience is not too much of a stretch, allow it. Deepen your breathing anytime you feel resistance.

Step 4

Stick with it. Eventually, the tension you first felt with this surrender will release and transform itself into a relaxed flow. This is the experience that you can transfer to a buildup of anger. Giving yourself over to this experience will allow you to see that you can have emotions and move through them, rather than being a hostage to them. Breathe into the tension, don't fight it. Remember, what you resist is likely to persist. Rather, allow it to pass through and out.

Step 5

Reflect on the experience while enjoying a postcoital cuddle (yes, we're making you do this part even if it is usually something you skip). You need to reaffirm the bond and find your way back to being equal partners in the relationship. But remember the feeling of surrender. Also plan to switch roles at a later point, so both you and your partner know the sensation of giving up control. Learning to do this sexually will also help you to fight fair the next time anger surfaces. It's not about giving up or giving in, it's about letting go.

Bonus Sexual Solution: Sexual Role Swap

THIS is a role-playing quickie that can also heighten your understanding of letting go by helping you to let go of your "typical" role. Here's how: Agree with your partner that you will play a role opposite to the one you typically play in bed for one week. In other words, if you are passive, become active. If you are active, be passive in all aspects of love-making. Don't be afraid of the new feelings these changes will generate. Give in to them. The idea is for you to start to recognize that there can be tremendous power in learning to go outside your comfort zone. If you play with sexual swapping, you not only will help balance the power in your relationship, but you will also learn that letting go of the role you think you should play is possible. This can transfer to how you deal with anger especially in cases where you tend to suppress your emotion because it's how you think you "should" act. Let go.

Chapter

WE HAVE TRUST ISSUES

L ove-trust. These two are so inextricably linked that you can actually turn them into one hyphenated word used to define the basis of the best relationships. You can have love without trust and trust without love, but you probably won't have a very successful long-term coupling without both being in place.

Think of it this way. Love-trust is similar to driving. Trust is the engine, propelling the car wherever it needs to go. And with a reliable engine, a couple can zip down the highway of life, like carefree travelers on a long-distance road trip. There is a certain degree of relief in knowing they can relax and feel perfectly safe together while enjoying the scenery. Think of it as relationship cruise control. Freedom comes from knowing that your partner will protect you (airbags included) and help you maneuver along even the rockiest road.

In contrast, when love-trust is damaged between two people, it is like driving a car with an overheated engine that will likely fail any time the pedal is pushed to the metal. A couple might truly want to accelerate their relationship, but chances are one or both will slam on the brakes because of the fear they might end up stranded on the side of the road. And no one wants to risk finding themselves alone and abandoned. Sadly, this jerky start/stop act stemming from a lack of love-trust keeps either partner from truly enjoying the ride. What's more, the underlying worry that the engine could fail at any moment also prevents the couple from driving well.

Building love-trust is more involved and in-depth than the trust required in most other types of relationships. The process is delicate and develops gradually over time. Certain actions or decisions may hasten or halt the formation of love-trust but the best results come when the acceleration is paced. In other words, going from "zero to 60" in a relationship is not prudent and could result in a love-trust crash!

Attempting to jump straight into a state of love-trust is like driving drunk; outwardly you may appear fine, but what's actually going on underneath the surface is a little foggy and off-kilter. A better bet is to identify what will promote or decay the formation of trust in your relationship and then work on gradually removing any obstacles hindering your growth as a couple. You need time to build love-trust and trying to force its development will ultimately backfire.

While love-trust means different things to different people— honesty, loyalty, responsibility, fidelity, reliability—at its core is feeling physically secure and emotionally safe. When you truly trust someone, you are able to express your deepest feelings and fears to them. You can also feel confident that you are free to let down your guard—revealing who you are, what you want, and what you need, all the while knowing the other person will accept you, respect your feelings, and protect you. In turn, if that person feels trusting of you, reciprocation will be easy for them knowing that you will respond in kind.

In essence, when you trust someone and act on that trust, you are giving that person a piece of yourself. You believe they will comprehend, care for, and cherish the faith you have placed in them. When they feel the same way and give you their trust, then you will find that you are both better able to be open and vulnerable with each other. That may sound scary, but in actuality the ability to mutually expose your inner selves will contribute greatly to the growth of shared intimacy.

Some people mistakenly think that tests of love-trust only come into play under extenuating circumstances, such as when one partner accuses the other of cheating and the other partner vehemently denies it (even if it's true). But love-trust is actually something that must permeate an entire relationship down to the most minute level. Partners need to be able to rely on each other in an all-inclusive way, and that means knowing their significant other will be dependable, honest, keep promises, act responsibly, maintain confidences, and return their love. Thus, while small, isolated breaches in love-trust may seemingly have only minor consequences on the surface, if these transgressions become a pattern, the cumulative impact may be enormous.

Small Things Are Big

You've probably heard the phrase, "It's the little things that count." Though usually uttered in reference to the remembrance of thoughtful little gestures, this can also translate to love-trust, and the growth or erosion thereof.

The painful truth is that, by and large, our love partners probably disappoint us more often as a result of everyday misunderstandings than by serious soap opera–worthy betrayals. Remember, trust is built over time so while one cataclysmic event can definitely destroy a relationship, tiny little chips in your love-trust fortress can also weaken your foundation as a couple.

So what kinds of "little" things are being discussed here? Well, consider the case of Dan and Laura. Dan's background is, in a word, colorful, and Laura has made it clear that some of his drinking, smoking, swearing friends are really not the best influence on him. One friend in particular, Bobby, always seems to lure Dan into precarious situations so Laura asked Dan not to see him for the sake of their marriage. Dan agreed. However, he's still hanging out with his friend in secret:

EVEN though I told Laura I wouldn't see Bobby, I do still make plans with him. It just seemed easier to pretend that I wouldn't see him than to argue with her anymore about the issue. And I figure that what Laura doesn't know won't hurt her. If I tell her I won't see Bobby, she's happy. If I can still see him, I'm happy. So it's a win-win right? I just tell Laura I have to work late occasionally so Bobby and I can go for a drink or play pool together for a while. Nonetheless, if I told Laura, she would flip out, so why aggravate her?

Why aggravate her? What Dan doesn't seem to realize is that he's not protecting Laura with his subversive behavior or "making her happy." He's lying to her! It definitely makes you wonder what else Dan might hide in order to avoid confrontation with

Laura. Imagine what would happen if Laura were to discover Dan's intentional fibbing.

This is one of many types of deception that can undermine a relationship. If Laura ever does find out that Dan is sneaking off to see Bobby, there will be a huge chink in their love-trust. She'll probably find herself questioning Dan every time he comes home from work late, or find herself feeling compelled to check his phone records. His "friend affair," though not romantic in nature, could have a huge impact on his love relationship if it comes to light.

Are you starting to see how even "small" transgressions can have a larger cumulative effect on a couple's love-trust? It is the repercussions of such actions that magnify any breach of trust, no matter how minor they might seem on the surface.

Frequent Fibbers

No, really. You don't look fat in that outfit. Sound familiar? What about, *Of course I want to have sex with you all the time.* Or maybe, *Since I met you, I never even look at other women.*

Yet another seemingly innocuous yet highly trust-eroding practice involves everyday pretense. Little white lies told in order to maintain the relationship status quo. The rationale in such cases is usually, "But I don't want to hurt his (or her) feelings." The problem is the recipient of such false compliments can usually see through these reassurances and consequently, that undermines the credibility of both the "kind words" and the significant other.

23

You see, while we may want our partner to be supportive, we also don't want to consistently receive falsehoods from our partner. If we can't trust our partner to be honest with us, then whom can we trust?

This doesn't give you license to be a jerk or to constantly put down your significant other in the name of "truth for trust." However, it is important to know that if all you do is feed your partner falsehoods, he or she will be hesitant to believe you when you're trying to give them a heartfelt compliment. If they can't believe what you're saying, insecurity will be more likely to set in than if you had told them the truth sensitively. It's a fine intention, but erroneous pretense will erode trust just as much as outright deception and lying.

Another serious form of frequent fibbing comes with gambling, drinking, compulsive shopping, and drug, online, or sex addictions. People who have difficulty with these issues rarely speak honestly about the extent of their compulsive actions and frequently engage in "sneak behavior" around their partner in order to try to maintain their relationship while still getting a "fix." However, continuous attempts to conceal the severity of their issues will unequivocally set the relationship hurtling down a pathway towards broken trust.

Consider the case of Pete and Tracy. After two years together, Tracy discovered that Pete was addicted to Internet porn and was racking up huge online bills. He hid his addiction by opening new credit cards (having the bills sent to work), creating a slew of online personas/e-mails through which he could log in undetected, and constantly siphoning money out of their joint accounts, telling Tracy they were for "purchases" he never made in order to pay his porn bills. And yet, when Tracy began to put the pieces together, he lied about it to her face (addiction = lying). What Pete didn't know was that with every fib he told to protect his image, he was also chipping away at the wall of their trust as a couple.

I remember the day I finally discovered the severity of Pete's addiction. He'd gotten careless and left his computer on connected to one of the porn sites he frequented. Not only was I shocked at the content of the site, but when I realized how much they charged for access suddenly everything made sense. I knew why he had been sneaking around late at night, why we never seemed to get ahead financially, why our credit reports didn't come in perfect, why he didn't want to make love to me as frequently. He was hooked on sex in cyberspace and then lying to me about it. When I confronted him finally with irrefutable evidence, he admitted to his issues and promised to get help but I knew that our trust was massively damaged by his actions. How could I believe he wasn't doing this anymore even if he said he was in control? I knew at that moment that my trust of this man would never be quite as complete again. It was a sad realization.

The loss of trust is sad. Since it's the foundation of a relationship, damage to love-trust marks the end of something beautiful and the beginning of a struggle to regain what may never quite be the same. The bottom line here is that it's not "his" problem or "her" problem when you're part of a couple. Like it or not, it becomes "our" problem. And if one partner is keeping information from the other, then the disappointed or surprised partner often feels like he'll never be able to fully trust his significant other again. That is the power of even the smallest trust betrayed. It spreads throughout the entire relationship like a deadly toxin.

Sex and Trust

Among the more sensitive areas in the love-trust category is sex. What happens between the sheets is particularly important to the development of trust between love partners. How many women, even in our current, more enlightened age, have kept the secret that they don't reach orgasms with their partners? How many men have lied to their partners—"Ogle? I didn't even notice her!"—in order to avoid a fight? And on the dating scene, frequent fibbing is even more common. It's not uncommon to hear, *You're the first I've ever done that with.* Or, *Wow, that was the best sex I've ever had.* Maybe, *I want you to be the last person I ever sleep with.* And most definitely, *Your body is a temple.*

The reasons for such false uttering—if they are indeed false—is that both men and women sacrifice honesty in this most sensitive of interactions to bolster their own or their partner's ego, or because they are embarrassed by their own "shortcomings." So they pretend. Unfortunately, as long as they do so, they are undermining, rather than building trust.

On the flip side, if a couple could discuss their feelings honestly and reject the myth that a mind-blowing orgasm or ever-charged libido is the ticket to self-worth; their sack sessions would likely become more fulfilling. Sex could morph from an exercise in mutual game-playing based on falsehoods to a true expression of intimacy. The latter is a much more rewarding option.

Additionally, the link between trust and good sex is so strong you can probably imagine how your sex life will suffer if your love-trust is damaged outside the bedroom. Sadly, this sometimes feeds further into mutual deception. Many couples whose sexual relationship has deteriorated seek help through compulsive pornography, affairs (male and female), and other misguided sexual behaviors. All this to ultimately find out the problem they are having in the sack isn't a sexual problem after all. It is a trust issue that has crossed the threshold into the bedroom stemming from the mistrust elsewhere in their lives.

The problem with these misplaced carnal concoctions is that they don't do anything to actually help the relationship. In reality, a couple may find themselves even further discouraged because the closeness that comes from a bonded, authentic sexual experience is not truly there and will not suddenly appear unless the eroded trust is addressed.

Repairing Trust

One cannot manufacture trust; it manifests. It is a result of honesty and consistency and it takes time. As individuals, we can choose to be honest and say what we experience and what we feel; by acting in this way, we indicate that we can be trusted. And although honesty does not always bring a loving response, it is essential for a loving response to occur.

Trust is something that comes about thanks to a concerted effort from both parties. Sometimes it is developed through a process of taking two steps forward and one step back, but as long as there is more movement towards building a bond rather than destroying it, love-trust can be achieved. When love-trust is in place, it can actually function as the crux that allows a couple to deal with a myriad of other relationship problems. If truthful disclosure encourages the growth of trust, trust in turn encourages the kind of disclosure that is needed for future growth as a duo.

So what happens when there is a rift in your relational love-trust infrastructure? Can it be repaired? Of course it depends on the severity of the breach but there are some things you can do as a twosome to restabilize your love-trust trusses. To begin your trust repair work, consider beginning with these basic suggestions.

Communicate and Confer

An apology from the guilty party for the trust transgression—clean and unmitigated—is critical. Following an apology is the discussion, or more likely a series of discussions with the goal of understanding the basis for trust violations. Simply stated, "Why has this happened, and what is going to happen that will prevent a recurrence?" However, keep in mind that simply understanding the basis for a breach of trust does not guarantee that it won't happen again. Unless there is a belief in magic, it is unreasonable to assume that trust violations will not recur without addressing the reasons they have occurred and formulating a prevention plan.

Ask Questions

When discussing the state of your love-trust, consider posing some of the following questions for discussion:

♂ What influences from our family of origin may be undermining our relationship?

♀ What changes need to be made in our relationship to strengthen the trust and intimacy?

♂ Very specifically, what kinds of behaviors are acceptable and what are out of bounds?

♀ Can the damage be repaired? What, specifically, will it take?

If you are truly interested in re-cementing your love-trust bond, then you'll need answers in order to figure out how to progress to the next step of rekindling your relationship.

Walk the Talk

While talking is critical, it is not enough. Behavioral patterns require change as well. In the past, for example, the partner who has violated the trust may have come home at night, barely mumbled a hello while reviewing the mail, made some small talk during dinner, and retired to the couch to watch television for the remainder of the evening. That routine, not much of a relationship promoter under any circumstance, definitely won't cut it in the wake of a breach of trust. Both partners will have to be committed to communicating and working together to ensure that there is a real-life reconnection process going on. This might include planning time just for the two of you, or perhaps initiating new patterns into your daily life.

Visualize the Outcome

The offending partner needs to think through exactly what he would like to see happen in the relationship and behave in a manner that promotes that vision. Regardless of the specifics, the general message this behavior should convey is, "I love you. You matter to me. I want to demonstrate that I am trustworthy." This may require a shift in the usual manner of behaving and in the daily routine; it can be a lot of work and may be a real stretch for some people. If you want to repair a serious trust issue, it can only happen in the context of a caring environment. It is up to the offending partner to create that atmosphere, even if it is at some personal sacrifice to them.

Support Baby Steps

The reparative behaviors required might be new and a stretch, but they do not have to be sensational. Indeed, some people are so preoccupied with major shifts that they overlook opportunities for small but important gestures. Others mistakenly believe that a repair process moves along on its own energy and consequently do not bother to fuel it at all. These individuals are the same ones who seem to sidestep escalating conflict by sweeping the incident under the rug and acting as if it never occurred. It may appear as if conflict has been safely avoided in these instances, but that is never truly the case. Appearances notwithstanding, there is no avoidance of trust violations without negative consequences. With this in mind, both partners should view any sign of trust repair, even the smallest incidence, as a positive step in the right direction towards the ultimate goal of putting a solid love-trust bond once more in place.

Now that you've begun the process of repairing your love-trust verbally, it's time to think about cementing that work physically. By remembering what it means to trust each other in your most vulnerable state (i.e., literally and figuratively naked), you can enhance your bond as a couple. We all tend to put up walls to protect ourselves from getting hurt, but when you trust that your partner will support your physical self in a healthy way it is easier to be open to believing your partner will also be forthright in nonsexual contexts. The following experience will enhance all the work you do, clothed and stripped.

Sexual Solution

The average hug is less than four seconds because many people are self-conscious about hugging and being hugged. Being held close is a primal experience that can be, at the same time, threatening and therapeutic. The experience is reminiscent of a moment in childhood that evokes a feeling of being cherished and protected, that deep feeling of wordless security that deepens the trust between two people.

As adults, too often we shield ourselves against experiences that can trigger strong emotional responses. Instead, we armor ourselves with defenses and resistance that shield us from experiencing things too intensely. The hug is a good example; instead of taking it in like a transfusion of security we break from the hug prematurely or stiffen from its effect, thereby blocking its positive energy.

If we are open to it, a hug provides us with a safe door to trust. And because it feels so good, it is an easily accessible reminder that it doesn't take a complete transformation to feel safe with a love partner. What's more, a hug can be very telling and is likely to promote the kind of discussion that has implications for sexuality as well as many other factors in a relationship, including trust.

THE MERGE HUG

This experience is set up to support the verbal work you've done already to repair trust. As you probably already surmised, sexual trust is huge! If you don't trust your partner when you're baring your body, then it is going to be hard to have an authentic relationship, no less a fulfilling sexual experience. Therefore, when rebuilding trust outside the bedroom, it's a good idea to rebuild it *slowly* within the bedroom as well. Take a step back from your usual let's-dive-right-into-intercourse routine and instead spend some time reconnecting body-to-body.

Step 1

Start by exchanging a hug with your partner. It doesn't have to be anything special; just the usual hug. Separate, sit down, close your eyes, and reflect on the experience. Take special note of anxiety, tension, impatience, stiffness, holding your breath, breaking away quickly, or any other form of resistance that you noticed. What did you notice about your partner?

Step 2

Discuss the experience, close together, facing each other. Share what you felt, both of your own experience and what came from your partner. Listen attentively and nondefensively as your partner does the same. Commonly, partners do the A-frame hug, with only the upper parts of their bodies touching. The kind of hug you may give a relative that you see only on special occasions. This limited hug with your partner conveys a "Let's not get too involved" kind of message.

Step 3

Do the hug again, but this time, with a big, sexy leap. Take off your clothes! Stand across from each other and make good eye contact. Now slowly, breathing fully and deeply, approach each other. As you come closer, open your arms in anticipation (no giggling!) and merge. Wrap your arms around each other fully; making sure that, from top to bottom, you are in contact with each other. The aim is not to squeeze each other, but to embrace fully, to feel as if you have allowed yourself to conjoin with your partner.

Step 4

Once you are feeling that you have relaxed into the hug, take it further. Allow your pelvis to move forward, touching the pelvis of your partner. Let your body feel totally tension-free in close contact with your partner. Breathe deeply and slowly. Notice your partner's breath pattern and gradually synchronize. Focus on the physical sensations as you inhale and exhale together. It will serve to transform you from two separate entities into one living, breathing unit. You may even start to support each other's weight a bit, which will enhance the trust connection (i.e., if you let go, one of you falls).

As you become more and more one in an effortless way, you are likely to feel arousal building. If you choose to express your arousal, do so in a particularly unrushed manner, continuing with the feeling of trust and safety established in the hug. The idea is to carry the feelings of trust developed within the merge hug into a supportive intimate environment if that's the direction you end up going.

Trust Merge Hug Responses

Couples exploring the Merge Hug may find themselves experiencing a myriad of feelings. Interestingly, when we talked to couples who tried the Merge Hug, their reactions frequently reflected what was going on outside the bedroom. Check out some of their comments:

♀ It was too tight, I felt restricted—and this is how I feel in our relationship.

♀ You were very receptive, and I felt closer to you in that experience than I have in some time. It made me realize that I've missed you.

♀ I could feel the tension in you, and it led to tension in me—I think this is what happens sometimes during our lovemaking.

♂ Our Merge Hug encouraged me to feel that we can safely take down our armor with each other. We have both built up these protective walls to avoid hurt, but it's possible for us to get through them since I could feel our mutual love and trust grow the longer we just held each other.

The thing to remember is that the first Merge Hug may be different than, say, the third or fourth time you try this experience. It's all predicated on where you are in re-establishing your trust. A good indicator of how you're doing will be when you are able to genuinely relax into a Merge Hug and feel supported and loved as a duo. In fact, at that point, you may feel the warmth physically spread to your heart. Once that portal is open, the path to trust will be easier to renew.

Chapter

3

JEALOUSY BUGS US

E ver met the green-eyed monster? You know, the one that rears its ugly head at the first sign of someone moving in on your romantic territory? Yes, jealousy is an innate reaction for anyone when they feel they might possibly lose a love partner to someone else. And like many other emotions, jealousy is complex. It's a combination of fear, anxiety, diminished self-worth, and a loss of control because someone else may get something we have, want, or hope to preserve.

Though the root of jealousy can stem from a myriad of sources—someone getting an object or job we covet, for example—never is jealousy more obvious, and potentially deleterious, than in relationships. Why? Well, when the thing at risk is the love of someone we adore and we see that love potentially being lured away by another person, it is enough to spark a full-blown anxiety or panic attack. How could we possibly survive the ego blow of losing our lover to someone else? The mind cannot compute the prospect of such an event and therefore kicks into high defensive gear, because at the base of any jealous reaction is fear—fear that someone else is doing better than we are, is more charming, more attractive, more successful, more appealing, and so on, than we are. The jealous feelings come from an intense desire to guard what we have, and that includes protecting our sense of self-worth.

Unfortunately, when jealousy flares, we fail to recognize it for what it is. We frequently make the mistake of thinking we must be less deserving or worthy if the person we love is seemingly no longer interested in us. That feeds the cycle as insecurity further breeds jealousy.

This insecurity may manifest as a result of lack of trust in one's partner and her commitment to you. In any relationship, there may be the underlying fear that one's partner will be drawn away and become interested or involved with someone else. However, when extreme jealousy starts to show up in seemingly innocuous situations, such as when our partner is just chatting with someone innocently at a bar or cocktail party, then we have lost confidence in our own self-worth. That's when jealousy can really start to interfere with a relationship's foundation. There has to be faith in the commitment between two people or jealousy will supersede all other emotions.

There are times when a little jealousy can be good for a couple. It can add a spark of intrigue, or remind two people in a relationship that their partner is desirable to others, which makes it even more special that they've chosen to be with you. In those cases, a little jealousy is a trigger—not for negative emotion—but for positive reaffirmation that you are worthy and special.

With that idea in mind, it makes sense to explore the idea that there are both good and bad types of jealousy and positive and negative ways of dealing with this feeling when it surfaces in a relationship. Because the green-eyed monster can actually be kind of cute . . . but only if the circumstances are supportive.

The Good, the Bad, and the Ugly

When it comes to jealousy, not all forms are created equal. In fact, there are definitely extremes. And while sometimes a little jealousy can make a relationship stronger, too much can lead to its imminent implosion.

The experience of minor jealousy here and there is usually not something to fret about. A fleeting bout of anxiety or fear that someone may attract your partner is normal and not necessarily an issue. This is especially true when you realize your fears aren't reality-based and the feeling doesn't linger.

Good Jealousy

So what exactly is "good" jealousy? While it might seem like an oxymoron, there is such a thing as a healthy dose of jealousy. Even in the best relationships we can start to take our partner for granted at times. On those occasions, when you suddenly feel a pang of jealousy, say while noticing a gorgeous singleton chatting up your significant other, that emotion can serve as a potent reminder of the things that initially attracted you to your partner. If someone else is finding him interesting, you might realize that you're still interested in him too (even more than you were aware). In those cases, a little twinge of jealousy can serve to briefly reinspire the relationship.

Jealousy can also serve as an indicator of love and interest. How so? Well, oftentimes people may not even realize they have romantic feelings (or realize how deep their feelings run) until they get a jealousy pang. And that little twinge serves as a wakeup call that they are more invested than they thought. In that case, jealousy is also positive because it ups the stakes in a relationship that may have needed a kick to move it to the next level.

The above scenarios illustrate how a little jealousy isn't deleterious and could possibly even add something to a relationship. Thus, should you or your partner experience minor, everyday jealousies, it's best to recognize them for what they are, even laugh at them, accept them, and then release them. Unless trust issues are also involved, chances are you can just let them go and move on (and even take them as a sign that things are still on track with your relationship).

The risk with "good" jealousy, however, is that things can easily change from it triggering a mild jolt of anxiety that can even be exciting or enjoyable to the more extreme forms of jealousy, anger, and fear. At the extreme, jealousy can become seriously debilitating and destructive to a relationship.

For this reason, jealousy is not something that should be toyed with. Some people play on their partner's fears and anxieties by engaging in little acts of seeming disinterest to make them jealous, such as smiling suggestively at a passing stranger on the street and commenting on her physique. Bad idea. Organic jealousy can be tolerated in a relationship because it serves as a reminder of emotional investment. Intentional acts of jealousy-invoking behavior, however, serve only to ultimately break down a relationship.

Bad Jealousy

When jealousy runs in the other direction, it will start to chip away at a relationship. Instead of adding intrigue or spice, it adds doubt, which is incredibly powerful. A doubt-filled mind is a fertile breeding ground for other relationship-wrecking thoughts and may lead to relationship sabotage (i.e., if a partner becomes possessive, demanding, or controlling out of fear stemming from jealousy, it will generally lead to the very loss of love they were afraid of in the first place).

How can one recognize the bad before it gets really ugly? Consider this: Any situation where jealousy leads to irrational, overprotective, or demanding behavior would probably qualify. A relationship fraught with jealous undertones might also look a bit competitive or fractured to the outside observer. Think about it: A member of a happy couple isn't usually flirting with others to make his partner take notice nor will he make a scene anytime his significant other so much as looks at another person. A couple without jealousy issues are comfortable giving each other a long leash in social situations because each person knows that his partner will find her way back to his side eventually.

Bad jealousy sometimes shows up as dominant behavior. It may also come out in repeated accusations, which is not healthy for any relationship. Bringing up something your partner did—like ogling a stranger—is okay once, especially if he wasn't aware that his behavior bothered you or made you feel insecure. In fact, voicing that jealous reaction may even make him feel good knowing you care enough about him to seek reassurance of his love.

The danger in repetition of such a behavior, however, is that it may become draining emotionally, or your reactions may intensify. For example, instead of asking questions about what your partner has been doing in an ordinary, interested way, you may start grilling for every detail of any encounter he has, which really makes you look nuts. Even worse? You might try threatening or confronting the person you believe, correctly or incorrectly, is your rival.

This would definitely be "bad" jealousy because instead of strengthening your position with your significant other, it makes you look needy and insecure and there is nothing attractive about that to anyone. See how tipping the scale too far can lead to relationship ruin?

Ugly Jealousy

On the extreme end of the spectrum is the "ugly" kind of jealousy and you can probably figure out what kind of situation that entails. Think jilted lover gone berserk or cheated-on wife who takes her husband for everything he's got. When it comes to relationships and sex, "ugly" jealousy probably gets the most intense. That is likely because sex is already a heightened experience; when jealousy enters the mix, the results can be devastating for a relationship.

A contemporary, fictionalized example of such a situation was in the movie *Unfaithful*. In this film, Constance, played by Diane Lane, is a woman in a solid but rather boring marriage who on a chance encounter meets a mysterious Frenchman. Eventually they are off on a torrid and passionate affair. Soon her husband, Edward, played by Richard Gere, starts to get suspicious that something might be going on. He has her followed and when photos of her and her dashing amour confirm his worries, he decides to confront the man.

At this point, however, the power of contained jealousy comes to light and he ends up murdering the man. Regardless of the outcome, you knew his life and his relationship would never be reparable.

While this is on the extreme side of the jealousy continuum, the point we're illustrating here is that jealousy is a powerful emotion that should not be underestimated. Learning to deal with it in a positive manner may be the healthiest thing you could possibly do for your relationship. Otherwise, the resulting fallout could be ugly.

Sex and Jealousy

As we already mentioned, sex is usually coupled with a heightened emotional state. When you throw other powerful emotions into the mix, there are going to be repercussions. A once-solid sex life that is now suffering from frequent jealous interruptions is a sex life that is going to be mired in either over-the-top desperation or perhaps domination, as one partner tries frantically to re-interest or control their partner. The problem is that both of these actions are likely to turn off their partner instead of getting them to demonstrate behaviors that indicate there is security within the relationship, which is what the jealous partner is actually craving.

How might jealousy show up? Well, consider the woman who fears that her beau is attracted to someone else. She might start acting overtly sexual or even start throwing herself at her partner more frequently in an attempt to make sure that he is still hers, or to let him know that she's readily available to him. Or she might do the opposite and start to withhold sex, flinging accusations at her partner that she won't sleep with him until he stops looking at other women. You're probably thinking this all sounds very immature but unfortunately, it happens all too frequently. Jealousy often causes people to regress emotionally and can lead to desperate actions that an individual might never even contemplate in their normal everyday existence. There is a touch of irrationality that shows up in most jealous behaviors . . . which could strongly resemble temporary insanity.

Jealousy also sometimes manifests sexually as control issues. For example, a man who is feeling some anxiety about the relationship may actually start trying to control this by being overly dominant sexually. It's a subconscious means of trying to convince himself that he still has this woman as his own. Unfortunately, in his quest for ownership, he may also push her away. Most women want to be sexually adored, not acquired.

The point is that most people don't properly direct their "jealous energy." What they do is spend their energy worrying and being resentful of their partner, neither of which is particularly productive. And neither of which will help lead to a truly connected sexual experience, which is really the only way to truly deal effectively with jealousy that has crept into the bedroom. Sure, it could involve playfulness and innovation, but the tone is about being real, not acting in a way you *think* will keep your partner interested. It is about your partner feeling you are fully there, not just putting on a performance.

Taming the Jealousy Beast

Emotional reactions to jealousy vary from apathy, when people don't care what their partner does (generally because they don't feel love or commitment), to the high level of anxiety and suspicion that breeds a hostile response. That said, jealousy is not something that you can just decide to make go away. What you can control, however, is how you deal with it.

Because people differ in what makes them jealous and how intensely they feel, they also respond in different ways. If you are only slightly jealous, it's entirely possible you may not even be aware that your responses are triggered by jealousy, and you may think something else is bothering you. If your partner is especially busy at work, for example, you may think you're feeling depressed, bored, or lonely. In reality, however, you might also be experiencing twinges of jealousy. Your emotions could easily escalate into full-out jealousy if another element is thrown in, such as your partner telling you she has to take a business trip with someone of the opposite sex.

If you begin to recognize that you're feeling a jealous response it is helpful to try to isolate the basis for your feeling. Once you've done that you are in a better position to cope in a more positive manner, whether it involves protecting yourself from a real threat, or taking steps to rid yourself of jealous feelings that are unfounded in reality.

Learning to positively deal with jealousy is definitely a skill that can be acquired, and this holds true whether it is dealing with your own jealous reactions or if you find your partner is displaying signs of jealous behavior. Here are some ways you can more positively deal with jealousy when you realize that the green-eyed monster is threatening.

Distinguish Fact from Fear

If you recognize that you are starting to experience jealousy that is headed towards the "bad," take a second and think to yourself, *How much do I know is fact and how much do I only suspect without solid evidence?* If you have irrefutable proof that your partner is violating the faith of the relationship, it's definitely time for a sit-down chat. Try to bring it up at a time when you're relatively calm (i.e., best not to broach the subject while you still feel yourself ready to explode). Avoid accusing, condemning, or otherwise passing judgment on your partner. A smarter way to approach this type of discussion is to make it about you and *your* feelings of concern and vulnerability, not the shortcomings of your partner. This will lead to a more rational and productive conversation.

Try Thought-Stopping

One simple but effective technique for curbing jealous impulses before they spiral out of control is called thought-stopping. As soon as you begin to think of your partner flirting with someone else, for instance, break your thought process by saying out loud or to yourself, "Stop! There I go catastrophizing again. Let it go." Then breathe deeply and exhale. As you exhale, send that negative energy out of you and focus your attention on something positive about your relationship. You can also try sending the message to your muscles to relax. While you may not be able to force your mind to stop thinking disturbing thoughts, the more you recognize what you're doing and stop the thought pattern before it gets out of control, the better your chances of keeping any feelings of jealousy from dragging you down and causing needless relationship friction.

Access Your Best Self

Remember that much of jealousy is linked closely with insecurity. One quick way to defuse feelings of "bad" jealousy is to shift from stressing about your significant other to focusing on taking care of yourself. This doesn't mean you need to go crazy examining yourself, or quickly hit the mall and buy a new wardrobe. What this does mean, however, is using this as an opportunity to focus on bettering yourself rather than directing your energy towards worrying what the other person is doing.

The point is that most people don't properly direct their "jealous energy." Instead, they spend their energy worrying or being resentful of their partner, neither of which is particularly productive. A better option is to take on the attitude (and behavior) characterized by being the best you can be, and accepting that it will either be enough or not. This attitude of "productive resignation" puts the locus of control back in your hands, rather than feeling disempowered and threatened by a rival. It is a serious and emotionally costly mistake to allow your partner's interest in someone or something else to result in a loss of your personal worth. Each of us has the responsibility to maintain our sense of self regardless of someone else's judgment or actions.

Even after a productive discussion with your partner, you may not be able to completely eradicate your suspicions or jealousies, but you can make a concerted effort to stop them from taking over your life. The bottom line here is that jealousy is like a defense to a perceived threat. But if you use that response in a positive way, you can discern if there really is any danger and respond to it in a manner that may strengthen rather than undermine your relationship. And this includes in bed. Keep reading to see how you can positively explore jealousy between the sheets in a way that will improve your sex life and your relationship.

Sexual Solution

Jealousy issues can be addressed in many ways, but in the sexual arena—usually the heart of the matter—the stakes are higher, and are likely to be far more exciting than a pointless argument. One way to deal with jealousy is to share your sexual fantasies about other people with your lover. It puts the jealousy issue on the table without really putting your relationship at risk. By learning to handle these feelings during fantasy, you'll be better equipped to handle them in any situation that arises for you as a couple, allowing you two to feel closer in and out of bed.

Sharing Fantasies

Fantasies have sometimes been compared to private erotica shorts running in the theater of our minds. Sexual fantasy is a nearly universal experience among men and women, with many of these erotic daydreams being nothing more than fleeting thoughts. Like the clips of well-made coming attractions, they entice and excite us. A man may glimpse a flash of cleavage in a restaurant when a woman bends to pick up a fallen napkin and may briefly imagine being with her. A woman may spot a sexy man passing her in the street with a flirty sparkle in his eye and imagine herself in his naked embrace.

Many people feel ashamed about their fantasies, especially if they occur during sex with their partner. In addition, partners often feel put off by sexual fantasies, worrying *Why does my lover need fantasies? Aren't I enough?*

If jealousy is an issue in the relationship, the underlying factor is a desire to be the one and only in your partner's life. Given this, is sharing fantasies wise? The answer is a qualified yes. The qualification involves your partner's sensitivity. If the fantasy is likely to be disturbing, such as the man who fantasized sleeping with his wife's mother, or the woman who fantasized sleeping with her husband's brother, this may be pushing jealousy over the top.

However, if you learn to share fantasies in a positive manner, you may be able to bring a new element to your relationship that allows you to constructively address jealousy issues in a sexual way. By letting your partner see into your inner sexual self and vice versa, it's almost like bringing another person into the relationship, but it keeps it at a safe distance because it remains, well, a fantasy. Once you've effectively shared a fantasy with each other, you will also get better at accepting that even though there may be someone else briefly occupying your partner's mind, you are still the one sharing his bed. This will translate to more security outside of the bedroom as well when you find yourself together as a twosome in social situations. Just because there are others present doesn't mean that your partner will stray. It's about knowing that you can handle temptations because your commitment to each other is solid. In that knowledge lies the key to weathering jealous feelings.

FREEING YOUR FANTASIES

While the thought of sharing your fantasy may make you blush, this experience will encourage you to open up to your partner in a meaningful way that will allow your innermost sexual thoughts to become shared territory. Not only does this help with open communication, but it also helps you learn to deal with jealousy constructively (i.e., when you think about your partner with someone else and can learn to let that idea go because it's only fantasy). Here are some steps for sharing your fantasies with each other.

Step 1

Discuss sharing your fantasies with your partner. One thing you should both think about in advance is how comfortable your partner will be hearing your fantasies. If, for example, your fantasies involve your partner's best friend, or someone your partner is threatened by, he or she may find that too difficult to accept. There's nothing wrong with stretching each other's comfort zones, but doing so also requires good judgment. In other words, make sure you're keeping your partner's feelings in mind as well (we don't want to make things worse by adding hurt to the mix).

Step 2

Boost your partner's desirability before sharing your fantasy. Reassure your partner that you have no intent to act on your fantasy. Some fantasies are practically guaranteed to make your partner jealous, so take that into consideration. For example, lovers who have aging issues may feel threatened hearing that your fantasy features a younger lover.

Step 3

Make it clear that by sharing you are not going to pressure your partner to accept or act out your fantasy. You both may decide it would be exciting to do so, but sharing shouldn't turn into coercing.

Step 4

Go ahead and share, but remember that sharing does not guarantee acceptance. There is a bit of a risk involved here. But just like with jealousy, the ability to weather the insecurity that comes along with sharing something that might not be well received is part of the growth experience. Your partner may not find your fantasy erotic or be at all receptive to your erotic short, but each of you is challenged not to condemn the other for sharing secret thoughts.

Step 5

Flesh out the underlying psychological source of your fantasy. Getting into the underlying issue, while provoking jealousy initially, is likely to defuse jealousy and the power of the fantasy. By "analyzing" the source of attraction, you are allowing it to be part of your relationship, rather than tearing the relationship apart.

Step 6

Consider what you have learned from the experience. Discuss with your partner ways that you can both accept fantasy into your bedroom behavior and don't be afraid to speak up if something he said made you jealous. Often in jealousy, especially when there is insecurity, the person is trying to change the circumstance when the real answer involves an attitude change about the circumstance. In other words, what is going on is less a real threat and more likely activating individual insecurity. This is the same situation when there is jealousy linked to fantasy.

It is always helpful when these issues come up to talk them out honestly. Real openness, where vulnerability is risked, is likely to create more closeness. In contrast, the typical response, blaming and anger, leads to alienation. Learning to share your fantasies with each other will help promote open dialogue about any jealousy issues you encounter as a couple, whether real or imagined.

Overcoming a Negative Fantasy Experience

Just like there are negative and positive expressions of jealousy, there can be negative and positive expressions of fantasy. Here are some positive ways to deal with jealousy when you feel fantasy sharing has gone a little too far and actually hindered relational progress rather than deepened resolution of jealousy issues.

1. **Prevention.** Sometimes a shared fantasy is a veiled hostility; it is shared with "malice aforethought." One person flaunts his or her fantasies to wound their lover or at the least to get a reaction. Bad idea. You might receive momentary satisfaction, but you'll pay a long-term price with inhibition in the bedroom and distance rather than openness in the relationship generally.

2. **View your partner's disclosure positively.** It certainly isn't a self-esteem boost to hear that your partner has eyes for the neighbor. You can retreat behind wounded pride or view his disclosure as an indication that you are viewed as emotionally safe enough for the disclosure to be made.

3. **Don't withdraw.** If you find your partner's fantasies disturbing, talk about it. Insist she listen without being defensive.

4. **Get perspective.** Remember that fantasies are only thoughts, not actions. The reality test is how your lover acts toward you sexually, not what he thinks about. It's about what happens, not about mind games.

Chapter

WE NEED MORE OPENNESS

When it comes to sharing, is your relationship an open book or a closed door? When it comes to communication, the couples who make it are the ones who are on the same page and know what's going on between the covers (you can take that figuratively and sexually if you'd like).

Sure, it's okay to have a few secrets of your own that you keep from the world, but do you really want to keep things from your partner? Ideally, wouldn't it be nice to be with someone who, as the saying goes, knows all about you and likes you anyway? Unfortunately, many couples forget that they're supposed to be a team and they find themselves keeping secrets from each other as well as everyone else. Thing is, if they were more open to each other—sharing their innermost thoughts as well as their beds and bodies—their relationship would be deeper and more satisfying.

Interestingly, in the beginning of a relationship, many couples tend to find that they are more open with their lovers. In this discovery phase, a twosome is excited and spending more time divulging their thoughts, ideas, and histories in order to establish common ground. It's a magical time, and talking and sharing is a part of the getting-to-know-you process.

But then somewhere down the line the honeymoon period begins to wane and so too does communication. This can happen for many reasons. One possibility is that comfort sets in and the couple doesn't feel like they need to share as much with each other because they simply assume their significant other now knows them well enough to automatically sense what's going on with them. They're forgetting a cardinal rule in any relationship: Never assume your partner can read your mind. If you don't talk to each other, you are setting yourselves up for future meltdowns. Share well and your relationship will thrive; harbor secrets and you'll eventually find yourself testing the strength of your bond instead of cherishing it. With that in mind, let's look a little at the importance of communication and openness in your twosome.

Just Talk to Me!

As we mentioned, in the beginning of a relationship when love is bursting into full bloom, communication is encouraged, promoted, and accepted. In fact, it's the very essence of falling in love. A couple becomes a couple as they share and learn all the little things about each other that make them unique individually and as a duo. Growth in a relationship is hinged on the twosome opening up to each other. Shared emotional entanglements are part of the fabric that weaves a couple together.

Once that couple status is affirmed (i.e., you refer to each other as "partner," "significant other," "boyfriend," "girlfriend," and so on), you might also find yourself getting lazy with the work it takes to keep that title. The test of love comes over time at a point well beyond the courtship and honeymoon phase. It is in the long term that the ability to preserve the vitality and energy of love is challenged.

The challenge of keeping up the relationship exceeds just simply coexisting. There are lots of couples who manage to get along just fine. The problem, however, is that some of these couples have also settled for keeping anything controversial out of their relationship. They favor the mundane in an effort to keep the peace. But with that peace, comes a price. And it's a steep one, because frequently the tradeoff for status quo is the "spark."

So how can you maintain the spark without neutralizing the relationship? Well, the answer is definitely not in keeping secrets from each other or attempting to hide your real persona! A fear of bringing anything contentious up in conversation will very likely endanger your sexlife. Why? There is not only a lack of connection, but there is nothing of interest left either. Personal talk has been exchanged for the mundane. In other words, "I'm really worried about my job" is replaced by "So, did we get any bills in the mail today?" The spark in a relationship actually stems from being emotionally open with one's partner and allowing the other person to do the same by creating emotional safety.

It's a two-way street that necessitates making feelings known when in conversation with each other while also vowing to maintain an emotional connection even when one's love partner thinks, feels, and believes differently. Trying to change or fix each other is a waste of energy, but truly listening to each other is never a bad idea. In short: Agreement is optional in a relationship; mutual understanding is essential.

Another important argument for striving to maintain open communication lines in a relationship stems from a study conducted at Baylor University. This study showed that a better predictor of couples that stayed together was not if they fought, but rather how they communicated, especially during a fight. The study differentiated between two types of negative emotion, "hard" and "soft." "Hard" emotion is associated with asserting power, whereas "soft" emotion is associated with vulnerability. The results showed that when expressed, hard emotion consistently escalated fights, whereas soft emotion was generally beneficial for a relationship. Soft emotion appeared to increase a couple's motivation to address a conflict and often led to productive approaches toward resolving the disagreement.

The point here is that hard emotion is more likely what happens when there isn't openness and sharing in a relationship. Hard emotion is laced with anger and soft emotion is based in understanding. It's name-calling versus resolution-seeking. A fear of not being in control or feeling insecure may also lead a person to suppress showing soft emotion, especially in the face of dissension. But by opening oneself up to showing vulnerability to your partner you may ultimately pave a pathway towards more connectedness.

Pass on the Judgment, Please

As we've noted, oftentimes the thing that keeps a couple from being open with each other is actually a fear of being judged. Partners might find themselves thinking something along the lines of, *Well, if I share what I'm* really *thinking at this moment, my significant other might not like me anymore.* This leads to the rather ironic phenomena that frequently individuals who have joined their lives are sometimes less open with each other than they are with strangers or other people who are not as important in their lives.

Why does this come about? Well, consider this—it is actually *because* a person is important in one's life that they might become guarded about what they share. This is because the view of people we care about matters more than just random others who pass through our days. The people who are there on a regular basis are central to our lives, and therefore we want and need their validation. It's one thing to risk disapproval with someone early on, but when lives are connected, the risk and fear of rejection becomes much greater.

The bottom line is that we desire understanding from our partners, not judgment. Accordingly, if there is any fear in a relationship that we will be judged for something we say, chances are we won't share with our significant other just because the stakes of disapproval are too high a risk.

Unfortunately, a relationship hinged on approval starts to resemble a parent/child relationship more than equal partners and lovers. Suddenly it's less about being able to tell our partner anything and more about figuring out ways to keep our love partner's approval while avoiding any negative consequences for "bad behavior." This is likely because the feelings of rejection and sensitivity in a love relationship are unparalleled in comparison to any other relationship we encounter in our lives.

That said, of course everyone gets emotionally bogged down on occasion. But when it manifests in a love relationship, this is more likely the result of an imbalance in which feelings are trapped instead of expressed. Just keep in mind that hiding one's feelings is actually more of an energy zapper than simply sharing them! And the more you have to work to keep thoughts and emotions suppressed, the less energy you'll have to be your true self and correspondingly, the less you'll have to offer a love partner. You cannot truly be present in a relationship if what you are presenting to your significant other is inauthentic due to the constant coverup of pieces of your personality. What's more, if your fear of being judged is so intense that you find yourself emotionally bogged down, your feelings will eventually seep out in the wrong direction or your defenses will become so rigid that the love in your life will starve from lack of sentimental nourishment.

Basically it all boils down to the fact that creating and maintaining a thriving and vital love, through the process of revealing yourself, warts and all, can be a frightening prospect. However, if this prevents you from taking any risks and being open with your partner, or discouraging your partner's openness because it doesn't conform to your views, you're taking an even bigger chance—one that could affect the longevity of your relationship. Such behavior will most certainly drain any relationship and ultimately leave it empty when conversation is reduced to the mundane since those are the only "safe" topics left to visit. The excitement of those early moments when sharing and discovery were daily occurrences will sadly become nothing more than a distant memory. This is so because the liveliness of love relationships, the very core energy of love, is fed by the openness that comes from the heart, which means talking about our inner lives, not who paid the electric bill this month.

Sex and Openness

It will probably come as no surprise to you at this juncture that if your relationship is suffering from a lack of openness on a verbal level, then chances are you're not communicating effectively in bed either. This is undoubtedly because sex is intimate by nature. So if you're inhibited at all when it comes to divulging your innermost thoughts, then we're going to bet that telling your partner about your needs, desires, or wishes in an open and honest fashion are probably not on your sexual agenda either.

Unfortunately, the inability to share and communicate during sex will very likely endanger your sex life. Even if you think you're "open-minded," that means nothing if you're unable to also articulate what is going on in your head before, during, and after sex. Remember, there is no such thing as a partner that knows exactly what you want. Some of it has to be verbalized or demonstrated.

This ties in heavily with the idea that many people are afraid to mention what they might want sexually for fear of being judged as deviant or prurient by their partner. Sex already puts you in a vulnerable position, so sharing while naked ramps that up even another notch (i.e., it's harder to hide behind a façade when you are unclothed).

Basically, you need openness in a relationship not only for a solid foundation as a couple, but also if you want your sex life to stay electric. Just something for you to ponder the next time you're thinking of not sharing with your partner. Is bad sex really a smart tradeoff for secret-keeping? It's your decision but the consequences will very likely cool the possibility of hot sex.

Share and Share Alike

So how can you promote more openness in your life as a couple? There are actually several things you can do if you sense that your conversations are becoming limited and limiting. As usual, the first step towards more openness comes with being willing to explore the issue, well . . . openly! Because so much of being open hinges on not keeping secrets from each other, couples who find themselves stuck in the land of we-don't-connect-anymore-the-way-we-used-to will not find their way out of that rut if they don't openly acknowledge to each other that their relationship is teetering on the brink of two ships passing in the night without either one sending out some kind of signal.

Therefore, we suggest bringing up the fact that you feel like you're not communicating in the way you did when you first met might be a good way to gently broach the subject of openness with your loved one. It's not about accusation. Remember, that is the fear-inducer. No one wants to be judged. It's about a desire to be a part of each other's lives in a meaningful fashion and that comes from sharing.

In addition to waking up to the need to communicate with more depth, you can also try some of these openness-promoting techniques:

Learn to Identify and Accept Your Own Feelings

One way to move towards more openness in your relationship is to consider your own "sharing" habits. Are you keeping things from your partner for fear of somehow being thought inferior by him? To be truly open you need to understand what you feel, know where that feeling comes from, and be able to express that feeling. If you find yourself at an impasse, hesitating to open your mouth, go ahead and ask yourself the following three questions:

☿   What am I afraid of losing?
☿   How may I be hurt?
☿   Am I afraid of accepting some part of myself?

Ask these questions any time you feel yourself hesitating to share with your partner and over time you will find that you can answer them more easily. Simply being aware of your feelings and hesitations will allow you to work through them, especially if you realize that the consequences of not sharing may be worse than just letting it all out!

Don't Be Afraid to Revisit Your Conversation

There may be times when your lack of openness is simply a result of not being able to actually pinpoint what it is you're feeling in that given moment. In those instances when you are unable to identify your feelings as you are discussing something with your partner, continue to think about it after the discussion. If you come up with afterthoughts, don't be afraid to share them with your partner at that point—later is better than never—especially if you finally identify something that might fester if not aired. Not sure how to restart a conversation? Just say something like, "Remember yesterday when we were talking about . . . " and you'll be off and running.

Create a "No Judging" Zone

If the number one hindrance to open sharing is the fear of judgment by someone you love, then it would make sense that creating a free-from-fault-finding environment would help promote openness between two people. How do you accomplish this? Lay out the ground rules beforehand. If you and your partner are having a discussion that necessitates honesty and openness to be effective, before you even enter into that talk territory, agree that you will both listen to each other's opinions objectively. It may be difficult, especially if you feel strongly about something. But if you promise not to judge each other and to listen instead, you are offering a kind of trust or even a peace accord to each other that will allow you to grow as a unit because of the comfortable space you've created in which to share freely.

Occasionally Play Twenty Questions

This may sound silly, but it works. If you find that you're feeling out of touch with your partner or you aren't sharing with the same intensity you once had, engage your significant other in a mutual game of twenty questions. Take turns asking each other things. Topics can range from work (maybe something like "Whom do you rely on for advice at the office on a daily basis?") to pleasure (e.g., "Which was your favorite time when we've had sex in the last month and why?"). Just playing this little "game" will open up conversations you might not have ventured into otherwise. And once things are "open," sharing will likely follow and become more uninhibited with each passing question.

As soon as you get the openness in your relationship flowing a little more freely, you may move on to sexual reaffirmation because a connected sex life will absolutely help solidify the verbal work you do as a couple. Openness and sex are a perfect intimate pairing.

Sexual Solution

Being open sexually is incompatible with hiding your feelings. Although sex is only one link in the chain of relating openly, it is, to most of us, invested with a great deal of importance. Women, in particular, often complain about men's failure, or inability to be intimate with them. They mean: He doesn't listen; he doesn't talk about his feelings.

Men, however, often assume that intimacy is what happens automatically when you have sex with someone. Often they don't understand why women fail to recognize what an intimate act lovemaking is if they clearly care about the woman outside of the bedroom (i.e., "Why do I have to talk about my feelings when I'm showing them?").

In reality, your sex life may benefit from both a little more open conversation beforehand and a little more uncovered connection during.

Eyes Wide Open

Eye contact can be very powerful—and it is very telling. Consider some circumstances where eye contact, or lack thereof, may convey something about what is going on. Recall, for instance, your family dinners when you were a kid. Were faces uplifted and animated, or did everyone stare awkwardly at their plates? Was eye contact natural and comforting? Or was eye contact avoided at all costs, especially in relation to some family members?

Then there is the simple experience of walking down the street. Eyes meet, people realize they're making eye contact and sometimes it feels good—other times it may not. This is especially true if one feels "undressed" or violated by the person looking at them and is offended, even though nothing physical actually happened.

When standing near someone in an elevator, most of us watch the floor numbers light up, rather than make eye contact. Eye contact in a confined space with a stranger feels too intimate. In other circumstances, the impact may be different; some of us, for example, have experienced the sizzle of "electric" eye contact with a stranger across the room.

Considering the power of eye contact, it is striking that sex in the dark with eyes closed is so common. On the other hand it is quite understandable. Many of us have to "tune out" to get close enough to make love; we don't want to be distracted from our fantasies of being with someone else!

We are never as open and vulnerable as when we allow our sexual arousal to be seen. You aren't likely to let your partner look deep inside you until you've done that yourself. If you're holding back from your partner (or yourself) when you're not in bed, you're not likely to act differently between the sheets. But learning to connect visually during sex can help change that.

LOOK INTO MY EYES

Rather than diminishing erotic pleasure, keeping your eyes open during lovemaking turns up the emotional heat. Some tantric sexual positions utilize this concept to help lovers transcend routine lovemaking to achieve a deeper, more spiritual union; so does the Kabbalah, a book of Jewish mysticism. Meaningful eye contact during lovemaking intensifies the physical sensations by deepening the emotional connection between lovers. Here are some suggestions for more eye-opening lovemaking. All of them will carry into your relationship and open your mind to more openness.

Step 1

Open your eyes occasionally while kissing. The visual stimulation will probably increase your arousal, as well as provide your partner useful feedback on how you are feeling about the kiss. Some studies have suggested that men bond more intensely with women when they make eye contact during kissing.

Step 2

Practice the eye lock. Look deeply into each other's eyes as you are caressing each other. Hold the look. Do this more than once. You probably won't realize how little you look into each other's eyes during lovemaking until you practice the eye lock. It may feel a little uncomfortable at first and you'll likely find yourselves wanting to break and look way. But the more you see eye-to-eye during lovemaking, the more you'll find ease in not shifting your gaze. This will further your connectedness and trust. Keeping your eyes locked will also force you into a state of openness and sharing with each other. It's hard to hide your feelings when you're looking directly at one another. This will heighten responsiveness to each other as well, since you'll get direct visual feedback with every move you make.

Step 3

Make frequent eye contact during oral sex. Once you've gotten comfortable with the practice of the eye lock, make sure to institute it in other sexual areas. Glance up from your partner's genitals while performing oral sex and make eye contact. Holding your partner's gaze while you're holding his or her genitals is a very vulnerable and open position. The impact can be electrifying.

Step 4

Look into each other's eyes during intercourse. The face-to-face intercourse positions encourage eye contact. This can be difficult for couples who are out of sync. It's also harder to objectify a partner when you're facing and looking at each other. Utilize the opportunities inherent in those positions. Don't look away when you feel arousal increase or when the connection intensifies your feelings. If one of you starts to look away, feel free to guide your partner's head back until your eyes meet and your gazes are connected. Avoid doing it doggie style for a while as it will be almost impossible to lock eyes in this position. The idea is to enhance your openness through visual connection. Turning away from each other will not accomplish this.

Step 5

Open your eyes during orgasm. Eyes-open orgasms may feel more explosive and emotional than other orgasms; the afterglow may be more tender and prolonged. Looking into your lover's eyes at the moment of orgasm is like an erotic gift. Even if the concentration isn't always intense, the practice is likely to generate greater feelings of closeness and spur more openness in the relationship. It will also help combat that inherent worry about being judged since typically a person does not make attractive faces while orgasming. Being willing to let your partner see you in that state builds security that you two will love each other no matter what the facial expression and no matter how you look. In the end it's about accepting each other with your eyes wide open, not somewhere in the dark.

Case Study: Eyes Wide Open in Action

LAUREN, forty-two, had the following to say about sex with visual connectivity. Her experience shows just how powerful keeping your eyes open during the act of lovemaking can be in fostering openness in a relationship. Here is her recounting:

When Matt and I got married, we lived in the hot zone. Passion was everything to us. We sustained a high level of pure physical passion longer than our other married friends did, but gradually things began to change for us too. He had the first affair, and then I had one. The excitement generated by the affairs, the tearful confessions and angry recriminations, the dramatic reunions made our relationship hot again, but we couldn't sustain the heat.

Eventually he did the predictable thing. He left me when I was forty for a woman half his age. Exhausted from being the drama queen, I went into therapy where I learned we could probably have saved our marriage if we'd been vulnerable and open to each other. But we weren't and I've moved on. My current relationship is different, better. Jerry and I are more connected to each other on all levels than Matt and I ever were. We read some books on tantric sex to liven things up.

The best ideas were the simple ones, especially keeping your eyes open during lovemaking. I'd gotten in the habit of using fantasies during lovemaking, and I thought I wouldn't be able to climax without them. So I closed my eyes, and had my own fantasies; I was almost having sex alone. Once I began keeping my eyes open, I didn't need the fantasies as often. I began really paying attention to Jerry, feeling and experiencing him in a new way, as well as experiencing my own arousal on a deeper level. It made familiar behaviors seem like new things we'd never done.

The eye lock, looking deeply into one another's eyes and holding the gaze, is the most intensely intimate experience either one of us has ever had. Initially, just thinking about it made me self-conscious, and it intimidated me. But I talked myself out of avoiding it. I reminded myself that there is nothing that bad about being self-conscious—it is an aspect of growth and letting my lover see more of me. Now I'm so glad I had that realization!

The first time I looked into his eyes at the point of orgasm, I was blown away by the emotions I felt. The orgasm was so much more complex. He had the same experience. Truthfully it took some time before I had the courage to do it. I never realized how hard it is to let someone you love see you that openly! Opening your eyes is the best way to connect soul to soul. Every time it happens it brings to mind how far our relationship and our openness have come. I don't know why it took so long for me to discover, but I'm thrilled that I have.

Chapter

WE'RE TOO STUCK IN GENDER ROLES

M ars/Venus. He said/she said. Masculine/feminine. North/south. His/hers. Bottom line? Men and women have different energies and sometimes that polarity can affect a relationship.

By getting more familiar with how yin (female energy) and yang (male energy) shows up in your relationship, you will allow yourself to grow into a more connected, communicative, and interactive relationship. And that balance will absolutely permeate your sex life as well. There is only one kind of explosion we want you to be talking about in that arena, and it's not the kind that results from an inability to understand each other due to polarity.

As if relationships don't have enough factors that influence their progression, added to the complicated beauty of couplehood is the simple fact that men and women are socialized differently. Yes, your relationship today began all the way back in childhood, when the emotional worlds of girls and boys are set. In fact, your interaction with your current love partner began to take shape before you could possibly have any idea that you'd ever want to kiss another human being. It all goes back to the way you were treated when you slipped and fell and scraped your knees. Were you told to be brave, or cuddled and allowed to cry? Whether you realize it or not, within your answer may reside many clues to your relational style as an adult.

While the typical social model suggests that women want a closer, more personal relationship and men resist it, the root and dynamics of this are actually more intricate than such a simple definition of male/female desires. With that in mind, it is wise to take a closer look at how early socialization may influence your grownup playdates.

Playing Like Girls and Boys

In most couple relationships, there are two emotional realities. While couples may exist on opposite ends of the spectrum, they won't survive as a duo if they don't at least recognize and respect the fact that sometimes it is just in the very nature of men and women to react differently to the same circumstance. It can be blamed partially on biology, partially on sociology, and partially on psychology. Whatever the "ology," however, even in the best relationships, there are bound to be divergences. Men and women are wired differently. And this isn't something that happened overnight.

Most researchers concede that boys and girls are raised differently. Even when the goal is equality of treatment and opportunity, it's just a simple fact that little guys and gals are taught different skills, rewarded for diverse acts, and offered varying emotional responses to the same scenarios. Consider the following: A shy little girl is considered cute; a shy boy is thought of as weak and timid. A frightened girl is protected; a boy is told to be brave or to act like a man. Girls are allowed to weep; if a boy cries it's usually done at the expense of ridicule. Girls are encouraged to be touchy-feely; boys who even brush each other's arm had better be in a wrestling match if they make physical contact. If a little girl falls on her roller skates, she'll probably end up on a parent's lap; whereas a boy might be brushed off and told to get back out there, even if slightly banged up. But probably the most pivotal point for future relationships: Girls are encouraged to share their feelings, little boys are not.

These examples serve to clarify the idea that little boys and girls are taught very different lessons about handling their emotions from an early age. This divergence is not only obvious upon adulthood, but it can even be witnessed in early childhood relationships. Boys tend to form playgroups that are competitive ("I can throw a rock farther than you!"); girls' groups more frequently revolve around cooperative endeavors (think tea parties and putting on plays or performances). If a girl becomes hurt or upset during play, chances are her compatriots will strive to make her feel better and dry her tears en masse. In contrast, if a boy is hurt or upset he had better extricate himself from the situation pronto or risk being trampled as the game continues without him.

Thus the pattern begins. From childhood, boys find themselves concerned with winning and self-sufficiency while girls are working hard to get along with others and create harmony. It's miniature Mars-and-Venus before they even know what life is truly like on Earth!

Once "vive la difference" kicks in and these boys start to notice the girls and vice versa, that's when evidence of these socialization divergences start to become evident to the members of the opposite sex. Suddenly "I just don't understand him" pops out of a teenage girl's mouth and the boy mutters something about "Why does she always want to know how I'm feeling about us?" for the first time. And a new verbal dynamic is realized that will probably be a part of their vernacular for the rest of their lives.

So how does this early play as girls and boys translate into adult play? Well, chances are once the grownups start playing with each other emotionally and sexually, the polarities of their interactions may manifest in misinterpretations or misunderstandings simply because of the way they've been socialized to conduct themselves within the constructs of a relationship, platonic or otherwise. Women learn to conduct themselves with compassion and strive for cooperation and understanding; men have been guided to "just deal" with things internally without sharing and have been lauded for independence and power. Of course, these are the extremes. In reality there is probably a varying scale and where you fall on the female/male or yin/yang continuum can shift from day to day or even moment to moment. But even with a sliding scale, there will likely be some degree of polarity in any relationship between a man and a woman just as a result of their genetic code coupled with upbringing. By and large, research supports these generalizations.

He Said/She Said Science

Many studies have been done on communication styles and couples. The thing is every couple will have their own unique interactive pattern predicated on where on the yin/yang scale their personal energies lie. However, even if a woman tends to have more masculine yang to her than the norm, and conversely, a male more feminine yin, there will still be some give-and-take patterns consistent with mainstream male/female roles in interpersonal interaction.

On that note, the ability of men to handle their emotions has become a topic of much social research and the findings are quite indicative of a gender disparity. In fact, one study by Vanderbilt University psychologist Ann Kring found that men and women may not actually be that different in their ability to *feel* emotions; the difference occurs when it comes to showing emotions. Women are unequivocally the sex more likely to express rather than repress. Put in lay terms, a couple may both be moved by a tearjerker movie, but it'll more likely be the woman reaching for the box of Kleenex.

What this indicates is that both genders are able to feel similarly, but what they've been socialized to believe is "normal" behavior for their sex may be reflected in their ability to share that emotion. And in the majority of cases, it is the male who will not risk the vulnerability that goes hand-in-hand with showing emotions to the world. Remember, men are taught to be competitive and get back in the game with nary a tear whereas women are allowed to cry a little and give/receive nurturing in the face of sadness or happiness alike. This tendency does not disappear with age. Even if a man wants to show more of his classically feminine yin side, his deeply ingrained mannerisms from childhood may prevent him from doing so easily.

Another study stemming from work at the University of California at Berkeley showed similar results. After studying 150 couples in long-term marriages, researchers discovered that the men uniformly found it more uncomfortable and even unbearable to become upset when faced with a disagreement. On the flip side, the women did not mind getting into emotional states with their significant others. Why? Most likely because they've been socialized to deal with their emotions more openly for years. To them there is nothing wrong with showing a little yin. For a man, however, this vulnerability may send him fleeing to the polar end of yang in an effort to restore his equilibrium.

And there may actually be a physiological reason that men are more likely to eschew emotional entanglements as well. John Gottman, a psychologist at the University of Washington, discovered that men experience emotional flooding at lower levels than women do. What this means is that when faced with an intense emotional interaction, men secrete more adrenaline into their bloodstream and when they find themselves in this heightened state, they are ill-equipped to handle the "flood" and take longer to recover from this sudden surge than do females.

Ironically, if they withdraw (as so many men do when faced with emotionally charged situations), Gottman's research demonstrates that their heart rates drop by about ten beats per minute, giving them a sense of relief that reinforces this typically yang behavior. Unfortunately, increasing the yin/yang polarity even further is the finding that when a man withdraws, a woman's heart rate increases!

With this in mind, it is not hard to surmise that one of the reasons men may shirk emotional entanglement is that they are not sure where it is going to lead (meaning it makes them feel out of control) and the only way they can handle this insecurity is to bolt since they absolutely want to avoid feeling emotionally flooded. The ensuing tango is comprised of a man moving away, trying to effectively sidestep his emotions, while his female partner follows in an effort to keep him from running. When you look at the classical yin/yang effect of this dance, you can see how each partner is attempting to position him- or herself more comfortably within the confines of a move they already know rather than trying to learn new steps in order to effectively dance with each other (i.e., it takes two to tango—physically and emotionally). Unfortunately this mismatched game of lead/follow will only serve to solidify a distancer/pursuer pattern that will find a couple trampling on each other's toes while not getting any of the steps right.

While there are differences between the sexes that widen the gulf between men and women on the yin/yang scale, there is also a side to this that both sexes experience. Learning to access more of both planes will allow a couple to emotionally connect on a level that goes deeper than weird science.

Yin/Yang and Sex

So what happens in bed when the yin and the yang of a relationship are totally out of whack? Well, for example, a male with too much yang going on may get too sexually dominant (remember, boys are schooled to be competitive and seek power in their early play interactions) while a woman in this situation may start to feel used and confused by his dominance (because she was socialized to promote harmonious and loving interactions at all times). See how this might set up some sexual miscommunications? Just from the differing understanding of the rules of play, one partner could potentially end up with hurt feelings.

The problem with an unbalanced yin and yang relationship in bed is that in order for a sexual relationship to be fulfilling for both partners there must be some reciprocity. There are, of course, extremes like in the world of sadomasochistic (S&M) sex where people choose to inhabit predominately one role and it's usually on the far end of yin or yang. In those cases where it works, the choice has been mutually agreed upon and serves both parties. Problems arise, however, when such a dynamic is unwittingly entered into perhaps because of an individual's socialization or unspoken personal understanding of the power exchange in a relationship. What may happen in such a situation is that the male will try to assert his yang personality too strongly and the female will fight back with her natural yin tendency. The result is sexual incongruity.

The best sexual relationships are those which tend to find their way to a balance of yin and yang. This can happen either through both parties meeting somewhere in the middle (we could call this "ying" or "yan"), where they allow their natural tendency to be combined with their partner's in order to reach a common sexual ground. Or, this could happen through the regular exchange of roles (i.e., "Who's on top this time, honey?"). Whatever the case, remembering that a relationship is a partnership will help a man and a woman negotiate their opposing sexual energies more effectively. It's not about fighting each other in bed or competing or even cooperating all the time. It's about balance. Remember the most evolved humans in Eastern philosophy have a proportionate amount of yin and yang so as to remain in constant equilibrium. You should strive to send your sex life to this same "enlightened" state.

Gender Resynchronization

It comes down to this: By way of varying social conditioning and quite likely differing biological wiring, men and woman frequently deal with their emotional lives in a manner that creates frustration as a result of a yin/yang polarity. Therefore, if a male/female relationship is going to be successful on an emotional level, men are going to have to stretch, since by way of socialization and biology they are not naturally suited for making feelings the basis of their interaction. At the same time, women must also stretch, primarily by not taking the difference in this important aspect of their relationship personally. It is not about what he did or what she said, it is about the different ways men and women interact. The point to take away here is that it is not that men don't want closeness and women do. It is more likely that they simply approach closeness differently.

But a couple can learn to readjust their yin/yang polarity, bringing themselves closer together on the continuum. It's about having openness to one's opposing energy, and being willing to integrate both sides of one's personality in an effort to better understand yourself and your partner. Here are some suggestions for recalibrating your antipodean energies:

If There Is a Yang Overload, Try to Bring Feelings into the Equation

Men tend to report on their experiences much like a journalist would relay news. For example, when talking about his day, a man might mention that he had a couple of meetings, he had lunch at the deli, and he took a coffee break at 4 P.M. but he might never once mention how he felt when his boss called him to offer praise for a job well done or how sad it made him when he was required to fire someone. Yet those emotional underpinnings of his day are exactly the kind of thing he needs to bring to the table in order not only to get in touch with his own more emotional side, but also to allow his yin-dominant companion to better understand him. For men, it is essential to ask yourself, *How do I feel about what has happened?* Then bring those feelings into the discussion on a regular basis.

Yang Partners Need to Refrain from Heading Straight for Problem Solving

Men tend to want to fix things, not analyze and discuss the motives or emotions behind an issue. However, they must be careful not to be heavy-handedly yang and short-circuit a conversation with their more yin partner by prematurely offering practical advice (unless of course, she asks for it straight away!). More typically, however, a woman places greater importance on the experience of feeling understood. Therefore, women might think that the offering up of a solution too early in a discussion is indicative of impatience or an outright dismissal of her feelings. Most importantly, women want to feel (as do men, when they think about it) that their feelings are acknowledged and valid. Therefore, a man should practice asking his partner how an issue might make her feel rather than just diving into ways they can solve it and move on. The more he asks for an emotional status report, the more he'll start to recognize its importance in decision-making and resolution.

Yin-Centric Partners Need to Remember to Exert Some Emotional Control

Women need to remember that men are socialized differently. Accordingly, those "shake it off" messages they got as boys may now translate into them being unequipped to handle strong emotional outbursts from their partners as adults. It's not how they were taught to behave in such situations and they will definitely close down if an emotional explosion is critical and directed at them. A better bet for the yin-feeling-oriented woman is to make a purposeful effort to calm down before any discussions with her yang-oriented partner if she wants to be heard. This is not to suggest clamping down on one's feelings, but rather just taking a time out until she feels some emotional equilibrium before tackling a hot issue. A yin-partner who is feeling overemotional should remove herself from the situation and then logically ask herself what the issue at hand boils down to. She already knows how she feels about it, but does she know what she wants to propose doing about it? A little breather will help with clarity and that will make for a smarter, less emotionally tinted approach.

Think Brevity When Adding Yin to the Mix

If a yin-dominant personality has strong emotions and lets them all fly without hitting the edit button, chances are that her yang partner will react by becoming defensive or shutting down (which is the opposite of what the yin actually desires by sharing her emotions). One way to deal with this is to work on being more succinct when relating the details of one's emotional state. Although all of the details may be important to you, a yang energy individual is more likely going to listen if the emotional point is

77

made quickly and in a manner that is less hysterical and more pragmatic (which allows for emotional problem solving—the best of the yin and yang worlds).

Learn to Share Yin and Yang Stereotypical Chores

According to separate research conducted in the "love labs" of Dr. John Gottman at the University of Washington, when men contribute more domestic labor, their significant others may be more likely to get "in the mood." This is speculated to be because women interpret their partner's domestic contributions as a sign of love and caring and are therefore more sexually attracted to their mates. But there is another hypothesis that we'd like to point out as well and that is that the balancing of yin and yang even down to the most mundane things such as household chores may actually help to recalibrate the ratio of yin and yang in a relationship to the point that a couple may find themselves drifting closer together on the continuum. Remember, understanding each other's energy will help pull you closer as a balanced unit. And this will definitely manifest in sexual compatibility as well.

Sexual Solution

While current research suggests that there are inherent differences between men and women, and that some of it is hard-wired, it is apparent that culture influences our sense of what it means to be a man or a woman as well. Most of us believe that there are gender rules that we must follow, and we do—but we can teach ourselves to break the rules selectively.

Overstepping the images of what we call feminine and masculine can feel awkward, and maybe even risky. Many men for example, feel vulnerable when expressing their feminine side, and many women feel they have to act sexy in order to be lovable. In the sexual realm many women worry that taking initiative and being direct about their sexual needs will put men off, that they will damage their feminine image.

Men, in contrast, feel that gentleness and being the responder rather than the initiator somehow is soft, less manly, and not sexy. After all, the cultural rules—unwritten, but influential—are that men initiate and women respond.

In reality, however, each of us can expand our gender identity, recognizing both the male and female aspects of our personality and thereby broadening our ways of responding to each other, both in the kitchen and, as a bonus, in the bedroom as well. Rather than viewing our gender behavior as a polarity, exclusively male or female, we can approach our lovemaking by thinking about ourselves as having a dominant and a recessive aspect to our personality.

By loosening the typical gender rules in the bedroom we will create a balance, an inner partnership between the male and female aspects within each of us. In turn, that balance will have a payoff outside of the bedroom. Issues that formerly were mired in rigid male/female responses will soften and more likely yield to resolution.

THE YIN/YANG GAME OF ROLE REVERSAL

In keeping with the Taoist definition of the male aspect of our nature being yang and the female aspect being yin, the following "sex-periential" yin/yang game will challenge your inhibitions while also allowing you to experience a broader range of sexual pleasures than you have in the past. The game will also provide training in drawing on your recessive side, male or female, that you will then mutually be able to apply to your relationship as a whole.

Step 1

Grab your partner, a piece of paper, and a pen. To start the game, go to a quiet place away from each other and make a list titled, *What I'd Want (and How I'd Act) Sexually If I Were My Partner.* Make a complete list of your wishes as if you were your partner, and how you would approach your wishes. Review your list and set up priorities based on feasibility (i.e., which of these yin or yang wishes could you and would you actually want to enact?).

Step 2

Prepare to share. Reconvene with your partner and decide who is to go first. Then read your lists aloud to each other. Some possibilities from the male partner's list developed from what he would imagine the yin (female) perspective to be could include things like:

1. I want to lie down in front of the fireplace and have you lick me, beginning with my face and slowly working down to my vagina, with special attention to my clitoris.
2. Seduce me spontaneously and take me gently, but firmly.
3. Make love to me slowly and sensually, kissing me generously throughout.

On the female side of the equation, some possibilities she might imagine from the male (yang) perspective would include:

1. I want you to slowly strip in front of me, one article of clothing at a time and then straddle me naked before aggressively kissing me, pinning my hands down, and riding me with abandon until I can't do anything but reach release.
2. Pounce on me the minute I walk in the door, aggressively removing my pants as if you cannot wait another minute to have me and then forcefully insert my penis into you for a passionate quickie.
3. Get on your knees in a submissive position and pleasure me orally while allowing me to pull your hair.

Step 3

Try to hit the yin/yang mark. Be encouraging when the pleasuring and approach suggested by your partner is something that would be right for you and a sensitive guide when your partner is off-base. The idea is to educate each other as to what is a turn-on for your gender as well as to think of ideas that you might enjoy in your sex life together.

Step 4

Pick one and do it! If, for example, the male partner is to go first, he will then select one item off the list to enact, approaching and pleasuring his partner from a yin perspective. If his list has truly been generated from a yin perspective—based on his partner's female desires, and how she agreed she would prefer that those desires be approached—then this should be a very fulfilling sexual encounter for the woman.

The benefits, aside from a very sensual, pleasurable, sexy experience, and an exchange of roles, is that each partner has to get into each other's gender mentality to create and execute the items on their lists. In other words, each partner is putting "me" aside to get inside the other's gender desires. As yin, the male is putting himself in his partner's sexual place, and as yang the female partner is doing the same, putting herself inside the male mentality.

Step 5

Have a yang bang. Next time you two are headed for a sexual encounter, it is *his* turn to experience something off the yang list. In other words, switch it up. The female will then be responsible for acting out whatever male experience the couple has decided would best feed their gender sync exploration.

Step 6

Intercourse discourse. After the experience is complete, and after a period to integrate it (meaning you've both had at least one opposite yin and yang experience), both partners should agree to a postcoital chat session. Some questions to ask each other:

♀ What did you learn, and how can you apply it to your relationship, both in and outside the bedroom?

♀ What was the most fulfilling part of the experience for you?

♀ How did you feel being the giver and receiver when you were getting and giving gender-consistent lovemaking behavior? And how did you feel when you were getting and giving lovemaking behavior that was inconsistent with traditional gender influence?

♀ How can you make this a regular part of your lovemaking in order to find balance in your yin/yang on a regular basis?

Learning to share and meet each other halfway on the yin/yang continuum will do wonders for promoting equality and understanding in your relationship as a duo. It's not about striving for androgyny, but it is about creating a male/female balance both within yourself and your partnership.

Bonus Move: Role Reversal in Reverse

TO take the experience even further, partners can play the yin/yang game once again, this time with the male partner as the receiver of a yin approach to lovemaking—the kind of lovemaking that his female partner is likely to prefer. Likewise, the female partner will become the receiver of a yang approach to lovemaking—the kind of lovemaking that her male partner is likely to prefer. Interesting yin/yang dynamics can come out of this kind of "sexperience" as well. Being open to atypical gender roles will add a whole new dimension to your lovemaking.

Chapter

WE DON'T PICK UP EACH OTHER'S NONVERBAL CUES

A look. A touch. A gentle brush of the knee. Perhaps a hand tenderly sweeping a hair away from the face. You probably recognize these flirtatious cues in an instant. They are part of the subtle, and sometimes not so subtle, mating dance that is enacted in adult courtship rituals. But what happens when the message behind the action is not what was actually intended? When the nonverbal language gets muddled, it's as if a couple is speaking in foreign tongues.

Communication between the sexes happens on many, many levels. There is the outright verbal conversation aspect, but then there is also the all-important body language component. This is in line with the premise we've been trying to impart throughout this entire book thus far. You can talk until you're blue in the face, but you still might be missing out on a vital element of your relationship if you've thrown up a physiological communication barrier. If you're not paying attention to what your partner is saying physically and vice versa, you're not truly in sync because relationships that are all talk and no action implode.

So what is the definition of action in a relationship? Well, there is of course the part about behaviors backing up what has been articulated in conversation between partners. Then there is also the sometimes unrecognized component of all the nonverbal communication that goes on between you and your partner on a daily basis.

There is a large quantity of research that indicates a vast percentage of our communication with others is carried out on a nonverbal level. It's no surprise that studies have shown that even in the absence of language, couples in various situations continually "speak" to each other sans words (e.g., gestures, actions, facial expressions, and so on). When couples are in discord, for example, messages abound without their uttering a word.

Think about it. When you're stressed, you feel it in your body. Your shoulders and jaw might clench, your temperature might rise as your blood pressure goes up, your back might spasm. And all of these physical manifestations are going to be reflected in your posture. So why would it be any different if you are angry with your partner, or upset about something in your relationship? Of course your stance and even physiology will change. The trick for a couple, however, is to start to recognize these cues in each other because sometimes words are less telling about a situation than the coinciding physical mannerisms.

Body Logic

No doubt the body is smart, but it's also a bad liar. In other words, while the brain may say one thing, it's the body that frequently speaks the truth. Why do you think behavioral specialists look to cues such as eye contact and arm positions when discerning if an individual is being honest? People are capable of talking their way out of a variety of situations, but it's much harder to talk the body out of displaying the natural physiological responses that go along with certain states of being.

This becomes of critical importance in relationships because often, when a spoken message is coupled with contradictory body language, a couple may find themselves in a disagreement and not be sure why. They may blame it on a sixth sense or just a knowing feeling, but in reality, it may have been the covert message they picked up from a noncorresponding physical cue that gave away the fact that something wasn't right. An example of this might be when one partner seemingly offers support but does so with an aggressive body stance, or when one partner swears everything is "fine" only to do so with a completely closed-off cross-armed body posture. Confusion is a likely result of such contradictory comportment.

Basically what you're experiencing when words and manner-isms don't match up is mixed messages at their finest. When com-municating, the entire body comes into play and that includes one's vocal tone, facial expressions, and body language. Such prominent cues as strategic avoidance of eye contact, eye roll-ing, glaring expressions of disgust, clenched hands, and quick movements are powerful indications of negativity, for example. Coupled with tone of voice, volume, and pacing . . . well, you can glean a lot of information from even minimal conversation just by paying attention to the other communicative messages you are receiving.

Ironically, however, a lot of people don't look at those clues. But they should. The wealth of information contained in an inappropriately cocked eyebrow or hands-on-hips stance is vast and ignoring those cues would be a mistake for any couple looking to actually understand each other better.

Behavioral scientists have found that most people actually rely on nonverbal behavior to get their point across, but it is particularly telling as a means of communicating attraction or disdain in a social encounter. The face, followed by the hands and feet, are considered sources of the most obvious cues to the meaning of a communication exchange.

For example, if a woman asks a man what his feelings are about her, his response of "I love you" could be taken with confidence or insecurity predicated on how he postures himself. If he looks down or away instead of maintaining eye contact, she might question his sincerity. Touching her or even resting his head against her while he utters those words, however, would probably give her an added sense of security that he means what he says—these actions are very intimate and reassuring. Moving his open hands toward her would say something very different than clenching his fists and jaw (which might indicate he's feeling pressured and stressed while admitting his feelings, even if he means them).

His tone of voice will also enhance or detract from his believability. If he says "I love you" in a friendly, sincere way it will be received very differently by his partner than if he sighs and says those three little words in an exasperated manner that alludes to "Why do you keep asking me that . . . you know I love you." In the same vein, rhythm—where the emphasis is placed and the pace of delivery—also affects how a message is received. "I love you" said slowly and deliberately with an emphasis on the word *love* will probably feel more credible to the woman than if it is said quickly and sort of run together (which makes it sound like a mundane phrase that is just thrown away and not really an utterance of importance).

Finally, volume is another nonverbal cue that may add information to the equation. Volume frequently tapers off, perhaps even to a whisper, under certain circumstances. A lowered voice may convey caring, as when comforting a child. Carried over to intimacy, a hushed volume may signal intensity and sincerity as if to impart, "What I have to say is for your ears alone." Conversely, shouting "I love you!" may convey a jubilance that adds weight to its meaning since it shows the world that he doesn't care who knows since his feelings are that strong.

The ultimate point we are trying to make here is that there are *many* variables that go into the communicative patterns of a couple, and if you only listen to the words spoken but don't pay attention to the corresponding nonverbal cues, you are going to miss out on more than half of the conversation you are actually having together.

Sex and Nonverbal Communication

On many levels, you might think that sex is the ultimate nonverbal communication tool. But just like a conversation about love and your relationship, the things that go unsaid during sex and the miscommunications that may occur during physical interactions as a couple are many. You may think that your sexual behavior is saying one thing, but your partner could be getting an entirely different message depending on how it feels, what your body rhythm is like, the tenseness or relaxation of your muscles, and so on.

This may manifest in presexual behavior as well as during the act itself. For example, if a man suggests sex to his partner and she says "no," the meaning of her response can be clarified by the facial expression that goes along with her refusal. If she says "no" but smiles a sly smile while uttering those words, she may actually be saying to her partner, "Don't ask me, you idiot . . . just take me!" If she frowns and purses her lips tightly, her refusal may be linked to something else that's bugging her, possibly even a complaint about her partner (and her "no" is really a "*No!*"). If she exhales and weakly declines, she may be commenting more on her own fatigue and inability to find the energy to "get it on" rather than a lack of interest in sex.

What you can note here is that despite the identical verbal response being given, the unspoken body language relayed a radically different message. And, in each instance, it's also possible that her partner could take her "no" as a rejection in spite of the fact it might or might not be meant as such (though the word *no* seemingly implies rejection at face value). This is how words and body language can create confusion.

Then there is the "Shhh . . . don't speak" part of sex. Save for some possible dirty language or potential moaning, what usually happens between the sheets has less to do with chatting and more to do with body talk. This is why an ability to pick up on the responsiveness of one's partner is the key to being a good lover. If the focus is put only on verbal feedback, chances are your sex life will be lackluster at best. Reading your partner's nonverbal cues with facility will lead to more connectedness in and out of bed, but it requires concentration on something more than one's own pleasure in the moment. And it may take work as a couple because there needs to be authenticity in the messages you are imparting to one another during the act as well as an awareness of each other's body language. Think of it as sexual multitasking. You don't want to give up your own enjoyment by being hyper-aware of your partner's messages, but at the same time, if you are able to pay attention to the physical cues emanating from your partner while simultaneously striving for personal pleasure, your sex life will soar. If you're both satisfied in bed, then you'll both be more willing to give (which leads to a greater return for both of you).

Marrying Message and Movement

When it comes to communication in your relationship, one of the best things you can start to do as a couple is to try to be consistent with your words and actions. Mixed messages lead to confusion and misunderstandings. Frequently, a couple may not even be aware of the fact that they are behaving in a manner that is inconsistent with what they're saying. However, just the simple experience of bringing attention to the power of body language to communicate can help a couple to bridge that barrier.

To work on your ability to read each other's stylistic and non-verbal signals, you might try the following experiences with your partner. The goal is to develop consistency between *what* is said and *how* it is said. With a little cognizance, you can learn to give signals that are more consistent between your actions and your conversation. Try the following exercises in order to align your words and actions.

Read My Voice

In this experience, sit near your partner with your eyes closed. Removing visual cues will force both of you to rely on what you hear and the information you can glean just from that sensory input alone. Now, bring up a topic that has emotional value, either for your relationship or if you don't want to "get into it" at this point, then perhaps something political or any other topic you know you can have an interesting conversation about. The idea is to select a topic that you know will be imbued with some emotional importance. Focus your attention on your own and your partner's voice. See if you can listen as if the other person were speaking in a foreign language. Try to understand the message by listening less to the words and more to the emphasis, tone, pacing, volume, rhythm, and so on. Do this for about fifteen minutes (or however long you want to continue the conversation).

Open your eyes and change the subject. Now instead of discussing whatever topic you were debating, instead focus on what you noticed about your own voice and your partner's. Be very specific in your commentary. What was your partner's voice like? Strong or weak, clear or muddled, harsh or kind? Is it judging, whining, angry, pleading, desperate, hurt? Does this voice fit what you were discussing or is it sending a contradictory message? What effect does the voice and its stylistic variation have on you? Does your voice mimic this or take on the opposite tone in response?

You may learn things about each other (such as verbal clues that trigger an emotional reaction) which have nothing to do with actual intention. For example, there may be a certain tone in your partner's voice that automatically puts you on the defensive whenever you hear it, but that may not be what he was trying to impart in the slightest. Learning to "hear" each other in different circumstances, regardless of what is being discussed, will allow you to understand how you relate on a verbal level and what effect tone, delivery, and intention have on you and your partner.

Create/Dissipate Mixed Messages

In this experience, the goal is to highlight inconsistencies in what the message receiver hears and what she sees expressed through body language. To conduct this experiment, you and your partner will take turns expressing a sentiment while simultaneously canceling its meaning with some kind of noncorresponding nonverbal cue (e.g., a gesture, motion, facial expression, and so on). The sentiments, expressed in your own words, should include the following:

♀ An expression of approval cancelled by disapproving body language: for example, giving a compliment while planting your hands on your hips, looking down, and shaking your head (actions which distinctly signal disapproval).

♀ A caring expression cancelled by cold body language: for example, saying "I love you more than anything in the world" while looking away, turning your head to the side, and crossing your arms in front of your body.

♂ An expression of availability cancelled by a closed-off body signal: for example, offering to help with the chores, but making it clear with your body language that it's an inconvenience and you're feeling put out by the request to help.

Take turns giving these types of conflicting messages to each other. Be aware of how you feel as you send and receive these inconsistent communications. Then discuss exactly what you and your partner do consistently in your daily lives to cancel your verbal messages. You likely have mannerisms you're not even aware of that may short-out your communication through your physical postures.

After completing the discussion, share the same experience but this time match the spoken word with the unspoken signals. Discuss the difference. On a daily basis, be alert to the nonverbal cues of your loved one that express approval, caring, and availability and make an effort to keep your own body language and messages consistent. In so doing, you two will start to communicate more effectively because the messages you send to each other will be met with increasing clarity and will impart authenticity rather than confusion or insincerity.

Sexual Solution

Think your sexual signals might be crossed? If you're not communicating clearly outside of the bedroom, you're probably not communicating clearly in the bedroom either. And when you're intimate, if those nonverbal cues are being missed, it will likely cause even more distress since the highly charged nature of sexual interaction adds another layer to this confusion. That said, once you start paying attention to each other's body language with more regularity, you'll be ready to pick up on those signals during sexual play as well.

In the same way that you can work on homing in on each other's nonverbal cues outside of the bedroom, you can learn to pick up on your partner's nonverbal cues in the sexual setting with more accuracy. Also, you can both practice not sending mixed messages between the sheets. It's about communicating on all levels while on the most intimate level.

Remember, you're probably not going to be able to read your partner's mind but you may be able to get closer by reading his or her body. It's difficult to mask intense feelings physically, especially when you're unclothed. Something about the state of nakedness during sex makes it even harder for the body to lie. It's probably the closest you two will get to organic communication, so take advantage of it and watch your relationship grow on many levels.

Nonverbal Pleasuring

In this experience you are going to pick up your partner's nonverbal cues in a very intense sexual manner. The giving partner is going to bring the receiving partner to the brink of orgasm three times either through manual or oral stimulation.

The giving partner not only needs to pick up the nonverbal cues as to stroke and intensity, but must also be sensitive to back off when orgasm is approaching until, after approaching the peak three times, the stimulation continues through to climax. In fact, both partners have to be very alert and sensitive to cues, because it is very easy to move across the threshold from approaching the peak to orgasm and release.

The receiver's challenge is to nonverbally guide the giver to exactly what is desired, how it is desired, and once it feels right to continue the rhythm for as long as it takes to approach the peak. The giver's challenge is to pick up those cues and to be flexible enough to change up as the receiver nonverbally indicates a desire for a shift.

The biggest challenge is for each, the giver and receiver, to pick up the cues early enough to head off orgasm until, after three times approaching the peak, the stimulation continues to climax. All this without speaking a word.

CONQUERING THE THREE-PEAK — FEMALE VERSION

Let's run through the experience with the woman being the receiver and the man being the giver. The instructions are for the man while pleasuring his partner.

Step 1

Pick your position. Have your woman get comfortable, lying back, undressed of course, with a pillow under her head. Her legs apart, her knees flexed, if that's suitable for her, or perhaps her legs straddled over your shoulders, while you are comfortably positioned between her legs. Keep in mind that positions may be shifted as needed throughout the experience.

Step 2

Start slowly. While giving pleasure you should be aware that to begin women typically need a light, gentle touch and usually prefer a broad stroke covering the whole body and pelvic area before focusing directly on the genitals. Using an absorbable body oil to smooth the touch may also enhance the experience. In addition, you should be aware that gentle teasing around the labia, circling closer and closer to the clitoris is usually very desirable for women.

Step 3

Begin to amp up the intensity. Taking your partner's cues when it comes to touching her clitoris since it is very sensitive, start to home in on her pleasure center. This should happen in a gradual manner and you need to be attuned to subtle cues your partner gives off. It might help to take the attitude of being an "experimenter" in order to stay open to your partner's signals. You should begin to figure out what works and what doesn't. When something seems to be right, continue with it until you receive a clear body signal to change up, keeping in mind that means varying stimulation but not shifting strokes abruptly.

After an initial warmup, if you stay attuned, it is likely that you will find a stroke that pleases your partner the most. It could be teasing the clitoris; it could be a steadier stroke, a circling stroke, an up-and-down stroke, or some combination. Listen to your partner's body for the rhythm and direction. You will also need to listen to her nonverbal cues for the rate of your stroke (i.e., slower or faster).

Step 4

Rate her arousal. When your partner's excitement builds, she will experience vasocongestion—her vaginal lips and clitoris will swell as they become engorged from increased blood flow. Her torso may also arch toward you signaling the need for more and stronger stimulation as her arousal builds. These are pertinent nonverbal clues that you need to observe, just as you would need to observe changes in her facial expression, her body posture, and her eyes if you engaged her in a sensitive verbal discussion.

When the peak is approaching most women tend to breathe more heavily and move around more vigorously as they become extremely desirous of the orgasm and release. Pay attention to this and as soon as you think she's nearing the point of no return. . . .

Step 5

Back off! This is the time to slow down and gradually taper your stimulation before she peaks. That doesn't mean hands off completely, but return your focus to how it all started—more on the whole body and the pelvic area than on the highly nerve-dense and sensitive area, the clitoris.

Step 6

Rev her up again and again. When her breathing has slowed, and when her body signals you, begin the process over until she's near her peak again and then back off. Repeat this three times.

Step 7

Take it home. After having gone through the arousal/backing off scenario three times, go ahead and take her through to orgasm—which is likely to be very powerful due to the three prior buildups—and her final release. When she's finished peaking, go ahead and hold her close to you—if she desires—as it will help complete the intimate body language conversation you've just had together.

CONQUERING THE THREE-PEAK—MALE VERSION

Here are instructions for completing this experience with the man being the receiver and the woman being the pleasure giver.

Step 1

Choose your angle. When pleasuring a man, there are a variety of positions you can choose. Feel free to experiment here, but make sure that your man is comfortable and relaxed so he can enjoy the experience.

Step 2

Don't be afraid to manhandle him. Women should be aware that most men desire direct, strong, intense stimulation to maintain their erection and to approach the peak. If the stimulation is manual, use plenty of lubricant, and begin with slow, steady full strokes up and down the shaft of the penis. Attend to his body cues and gradually incorporate the strokes he prefers. As suggested for your partner when he was the giver, be experimental, change up on the stroke, the pressure, and the rhythm until you get the nonverbal feedback that you are pleasing your partner.

Step 3

Check his arousal. There are physiological clues you can use to assess where your partner is on the amped up scale. Signs to look for when your partner is approaching the peak will include his breathing (it will become more rapid and shallow), his testicles will draw up, his buttocks and legs may tense up, and his pelvic muscles may contract. At the first signs of his build toward the peak, get ready to. . . .

Step 4

Back off! Shift and focus your strokes more generally, including his scrotum, perineum, belly, and the rest of his body. Of course, as you do this attune to his response for guidance.

If your shift is not timely and it appears he is going to cross the threshold, reach behind to his perineum, the area between his testicles and his anus. As you stroke along this area, you will find an area that is less firm than the other area along the perineum. With your thumb, press down on that area firmly and it will set back your partner's peak. Continue to stroke your partner in a less rhythmic and less focused manner, especially avoiding heavy stroking of the glans—the head of the penis, which like the clitoris, is nerve-dense and, consequently, very sensitive.

Step 5

Rev and repeat. Start the stimulation over, setting up a pattern of more intense stroking to the point of high arousal and then back off as the peak is approached. Repeat the cycle three times.

Step 6

Finish the job. After the third time of bringing your partner near orgasm, continue the stimulation through to climax and release, all the while taking cues from your partner as to pressure, rhythm, and pace. It is likely that the male partner's orgasm, after coming close to the peak three times, is going to be very powerful.

Follow up with Feedback

After each partner has experienced an orgasmic release, integrate the experience by giving each other feedback. Recount the moments when the cues were picked up accurately, when frustration occurred because the cues were missed, and examine how the teachings of the experience can be effectively transferred to nonsexual activities—for example, body posture, breathing patterns, facial expression, eye contact, and the like. Discuss all of this in a supportive and loving manner. The result will be better communication in bed and out, and what couple doesn't want that?

Chapter

7

WE DON'T COMPROMISE

W hat happens when he said/she said gets tangled with he wants/she wants and he needs/she needs? Well, unless there is some element of "we" in there, chances are compromise is not the outcome. Unfortunately, a couple will probably not survive if they don't learn the art of give-and-take in their relationship.

By definition, a relationship is a negotiation. Just by agreeing to be together as a couple, you are hammering out a sort of contract that includes fidelity and commitment along with other parameters. But any two people entering into such an accord would be foolish to think that there will never be a point when one partner has to acquiesce to the desires of the other to make the relationship work, and vice versa. In order to sustain any semblance of accord, there will be occasions where compromise has to come into play.

Very rarely are individuals so complementary in tastes and desires that negotiating and compromising are not required. As a result, unless a couple has a good understanding of what they expect to get and give to each other, conflict will at least on occasion be inevitable. When an inability to compromise surfaces in these situations, mutual reciprocity is usually jettisoned and replaced by bitterness, resentment, and general unhappiness. As a result, you can probably see the importance to your relationship of learning to compromise with each other. It may be the difference between an all-out war or a peace treaty.

Fostering Fifty-Fifty

If you asked couples how they feel about compromise and if it is a part of their relationship, most of them would unequivocally answer "yes, and it's essential." People recognize that successful relationships should include elements of give-and-take. The problem is, in reality that unequivocal "yes" should probably more truthfully be a "maybe, it depends on if what is being asked will inconvenience me or if it is something I don't want to give up."

We live in a day and age where people can get what they want with the click of a computer. While convenience is a fabulous thing, this always-available accessibility also sets people up to expect that they can get their own way more often than not. Unfortunately, when people become accustomed to immediate gratification, it makes them less receptive to the give-and-take dynamic. And yet, the crux of relationship success still hinges on that principle.

While many couples claim to work from a place of mutual reciprocity, the truth is that most couples don't regularly employ an "exchange attitude" in their relationship. Or they say they do, but in truth they merely pay it lip service. As a result, their many differences with regard to food preferences, moods, sex, types of entertainment, sex, choice of friends, responsibility for household tasks, sex, personal habits (e.g., smoking and drinking), sex, employment activity (e.g., working late or on weekends), and yes, sex are a constant source of friction. Instead of working together to find a balance, they start to give each other a tit-for-tat message that imparts, "If you won't change for me, then I won't change for you."

In a concession-challenged relationship, problems frequently begin to surface when one person feels they're doing all the acquiescing in order to keep the peace. This then leads to hidden resentments, anger, hindered communication, and a whole host of other issues that can trigger a tailspin leading to a duo's demise. If both partners do not feel they are getting a just return for their efforts then the result will be a power struggle, with each partner fighting to reap his "fair share." Relationships have to be a two-way street in order to survive for the long term.

In contrast, those couples who understand and enact the tenets of mutual exchange—compromise, celebration of individuality, and compassion—within the daily parameters of their relationship are more likely to work as team players rather than as opponents when the need for discussion arises. By recognizing the concept of "scratch my back and I'll scratch yours," couples who understand the nature of tradeoffs are more likely to avoid unnecessary arguments over petty issues because they have developed the skills necessary to allow them to discuss their differences not as adversaries but as partners. The ultimate goal between two people in a love relationship should be to create a *win-win* solution. This is not big business where a hostile take-over is condoned. This is a personal relationship, and the best relationships of this kind understand the concept of meeting each other part way.

What this boils down to is taking on a collective attitude as a couple that expresses the sentiment: "I can't have everything I want and you can't have everything you want. Let's strive to compromise in such a manner that we each retain those things that are individually most important to us, while simultaneously promoting each other's well-being to the maximum extent possible."

Pursuing an "I win—you lose" strategy means risking irreparable damage to your relationship. It's the equivalent of saying to your partner, "I'm not asking, I'm telling you." You can see how defensive that statement immediately makes the person receiving such an ultimatum. In general, a both-win philosophy creates longer-lasting and more successful compromises than a winner-takes-all approach.

Sex and Compromise

So here's the thing—when it comes to sex, of course everyone has their own personal preference. Some people like it hard, some soft, some romantic, some violent, some frequent, some only on special occasions, some . . . well, you get the picture. And these preferences may not only change from year to year but quite possibly from day to day and even minute to minute. So expecting your partner to want sex your way all the time is not only unrealistic, it's sheer fantasy! Sex is about compromise. Well, at least a mutually satisfying sex life is.

If one person in a relationship has a strong penchant for a certain type of sex or sexual behavior and the other partner tends to like more variety, for example, they will end up with a sexual malfunction unless they compromise. To illustrate this, consider Eli and Katrina. At the beginning of their relationship, their sex life was passionate, romantic, and hot, but as with any relationship, after the initial honeymoon period waned, they started to fall into patterns and roles as a couple. Eli had always been very dominant sexually. He suppressed that somewhat in the beginning of their relationship, because he was working to woo Katrina and keep her interested. After he felt he "had" her, however, he made his sexual desires very evident and even went so far as to say he wouldn't want to stay in a relationship where he was compromising sexually.

This admission left Katrina very confused because what had once been a mutually satisfying sexual relationship between the two of them was now all about Eli's desires and dominance. She kept trying to suggest more variety and that perhaps they could intersperse bouts of more romantic sex into their bedroom routine instead of this new all-hard-all-the-time dynamic. Eli would say he was okay with that, but when the time came for sex, he would always revert to his dominant behavior which left Katrina feeling more and more used. Her feelings began to carry over outside of the bedroom as she realized sex wasn't the only area in which Eli was becoming rigid and uncompromising. Sadly for Eli, he eventually lost Katrina because of his unwillingness to recognize that sex is a two-way street.

Sex is in effect an intimate negotiation—a copulative compromise. You're bargaining with your bodies but don't think for a second that what is going on outside the bedroom won't be affected by what happens between the sheets (and vice versa). A couple must learn the art of give-and-take sexually, which includes making sure both partners are satisfied (and yes, sometimes that means you might have to go without something you like). The thing to remember is that you can't always get what you want, but if you learn to work together, chances are you'll get close!

Going for the Win-Win

When it comes to the basics of compromise, there are scenarios which hold up pretty much across the board whether the dissension that needs resolution is between romantic partners, businesses, or nations. When discord ensues, differences are resolved in one of three ways:

1. **One side attempts domination**. The likely result of this move is an ugly fight between partners, a hostile-takeover attempt or war.
2. **There is mutual or unilateral withdrawal**. This is what happens when there is a hideous breakup, a bad divorce, or perhaps exclusion or isolation.
3. **Compromise is mutually reached**. This leads to a happy outcome and reciprocal goodwill.

With this in mind, it's probably not hard to identify that a couple seeking a more satisfying relationship in lieu of constant tension (or even eventual separation) would do well to recognize mutual exchange and compromise as offering the greatest promise.

If you feel like your relationship is in need of better share tactics, the good news is that you can actually learn to compromise as a couple even if your dynamic has become a little lopsided.

The key concepts to remember are *fairness* and *flexibility*. Keep in mind you are trying to promote a "team" atmosphere here, not set up a me-against-you scenario. It is not about winning; it is about establishing a set of rules and an outcome that you can both live with. Sometimes that means you're going to have to be the one giving a little more, but sometimes you'll end up on the flip side. The important thing is to make sure that this remains an equitable ratio so you both feel like you're getting your fair share.

When you are trying to effect compromise there are several types of outcomes you can strive for and varying ways you can come to an agreement that will serve you both. Try instituting some of these techniques in your partnership and you will be more likely to find your way to a relationship rich with reciprocity rather than constant rifts.

Practice Mutuality

This is definitely the "you scratch my back, I'll scratch yours" approach. The point is that whenever you can, give something to get something. If you are facing an issue stemming largely from some aspect of your significant other's behavior, you will be more likely to effect a positive result if you approach the subject by also offering to alter some aspect of your own behavior. This works because most people find the prospect of change more palatable if we aren't "in it" alone. Basically, one partner's change makes it easier for the other partner to change. Sometimes, the mutuality may be in the form of one partner offering himself as the support or crutch to help facilitate the other partner's change efforts.

Meet in a Mutually Acceptable Middle

Finding middle ground is the compromise equivalent of meeting each other partway. It is agreeing to buy the medium-priced 24-inch TV instead of the high-end flat-panel HDTV or the low-end 15-inch version with VCR included. Or agreeing that one partner will limit her drinking to one glass of wine after work when the drinking partner would like three drinks an evening and the other prefers she doesn't drink at all. It's finding a halfway point that may not perfectly suit either partner but will lead to a reasonably acceptable outcome for both.

Promise Future Payback—and Keep Your Promise!

Another type of negotiating is one that is not immediately time-bound. This doesn't mean you'll hold it over your partner's head and say "Remember the time when I did such and such for you?" But it's more like you weigh the options together and decide which option is best at this moment knowing that in the future, the tables may turn. It's long-term negotiating for the betterment of your situation together. In this instance, the couple recognizes that if one partner does something for the other, the benefited partner need not *immediately* turn around and pay off the debt. It is assumed on good faith that there will be an opportunity for reciprocity in the future.

As with most idealistic promises, though, it works best under good conditions: well-functioning relationships involving a high degree of trust. If, however, one partner continues to imply or promise that he will do something in the future but never gets around to it, or one person has an extremely selective memory (recalling all her contributions but none of the partner's), relationship discord and bitterness will be the obvious outcome.

Avoid All-or-Nothing Terms

A major roadblock to effective negotiating is the tendency to view the behavior of one's partner in all-or-nothing terms. Demands for radical changes practically always overwhelm the recipient and result in a refusal. Instead, consider employing another strategy. Begin the "negotiations" by presenting an option that is less than your ultimate outcome, but is something you know you can live with that will also be more palatable to your significant other. To formulate this less-than-ideal-but-still-acceptable option ask yourself what you ideally want to have happen and what are you willing to accept at this moment in time. Later, if the degree of change proves to be insufficient, you can always renegotiate. However, since at that point you've already got the ball rolling in a positive direction, additional requests are less likely to seem overwhelming.

As you have now seen, there are many ways that you can reach a compromise in your relationship. And frequently, getting to that point was probably not as difficult as it seemed at the outset. It's about employing smart strategies and working together, because in the end, together is what being part of a couple is all about. It involves joining the "I" of each personality with the "we" necessary to be a couple. In other words, a smart coupling is one that is respectful of each partner's individual identity, while forming a workable "we" that fosters and supports both partners.

Sexual Solution

So, you think you're getting better at give-and-take outside the bedroom but want to amp up this exchange between the sheets as well? Keep in mind that any of the "negotiating" techniques we related in the above section may absolutely be applied when trying to find your way to a healthy balance in your sex life. But that's not the only way to solidify the tenets of mutual exchange. Compromise may seem at the outset to imply give-and-take, but remember, it's also about working as a team, uniting your energies for a mutually beneficial outcome. With that in mind, we developed the following sexual solution which will serve to facilitate compromise in your relationship through shared energy.

THE SEXUAL MEDITATION EXPERIENCE

There are several ways to approach compromise; most are common, of the meet-each-other-halfway variety. However, there is one way to approach compromise that is anything but common: the sexual meditation experience. Couples who have had the experience have suggested that when lovers lie together for 20 to 30 minutes in the bonding position, their streams of bioelectrical energy merge, creating a unified energy field.

Many men and perhaps even some women may read the instructions for sexual meditation and feel it compares unfavorably to the more usual excitement of active genital stimulation and rushed release. But bear in mind, this experience not only leaves participants positively energized and unified; it also allows men to contain more and more orgasmic energy without immediate release. For women it provides a relaxed, unhurried experience for orgasmic buildup.

Negative emotions, such as those created by a stubborn impasse and lack of compromise, block the flow of merging energy. The sexual-bonding experience allows the energy to flow and, consequently, sets up an atmosphere where creative compromise is more likely. With that in mind, use this sexual solution to free up your collective energies such that negativity will wane and positive resolution may begin.

Step 1

Think slow and steady. Begin lying side-by-side, skin-to-skin, face-to-face, with generous and slow kissing and caressing between lovers. Kissing and caressing slowly allows time for arousal and sexual energy to build without pressure. However, as is usually the case, the energy begins in the genitals creating a localized tension. Typically when this occurs breathing is rapid and shallow. To counter this and to allow the positive energy to diffuse and flow from the genitals to your entire body, breathe deeply and slowly, relax into the experience.

Step 2

Relax and merge. When the energy has spread into your entire body unite sexually in a comfortable position that allows relaxation to continue. An arrangement that many couples have found ideal is the scissors position. In this coupling the woman is on her back, the man is on his right side with his left leg crossed over his partner's pelvic area and her left leg up around his left hip. This position allows the male partner to penetrate in a very gentle, nondominant manner; it is as if the male and female partner are penetrating each other, merging not only physically, but emotionally as well.

Step 3

Move with the breath. After insertion continue to breathe deeply and slowly and move in rhythm with your breathing, slowly and deeply. With each inhalation visualize taking in your partner's energy and as you exhale visualize the negative energy of resentment and stubbornness leaving your body. Allow the positive energy of reconciliation to flow in with the brightness and hopefulness of a new sun rising up in the morning.

Surrender to the flow of positive energy and the disposal of negative energy as you continue to breathe deeply and slowly and move in rhythm to the pace of your breathing. As you relax into the peaceful sensations you are likely to feel your differences dissolving and your heart merging with that of your partner. Be sure to attend to the subtle sensations that slow-motion lovemaking generates in contrast to the dynamic and more physical penetration and pumping of ordinary lovemaking.

Step 4

Focus on feeling as one. Continue the slow-motion lovemaking, but feel free to intersperse it with stronger movements and more friction between genitals as is needed and signaled by either partner. Rather than focusing on orgasm as the goal, pay attention instead to how you're feeling together. As tension builds up once again slow the pace, control your breathing, gradual and deep, exhaling slowly. Feel the aroused energy flowing from your genitals to your entire body. Visualize yourself relaxing your defenses—melting, merging, becoming one with your partner.

Step 5

Find yourselves merged. After 20 or 30 minutes or so, your bodies will feel as one, as will your psyches. Stay united for as long as you desire before either coming to sexual and psychic resolution, or perhaps even falling asleep merged. Following this experience, you and your partner will feel as if you are team members playing for the same prize that is only achieved by those whose hearts are one.

Nixing "Wham, Bam, Thank You Ma'am"

MANY men are much more accustomed to rigorous sex than meditative, slow, connected sex. Interestingly, while women usually go along with the former, a male partner might find his significant other more responsive sexually if he also explored the feeling of truly merging with his partner on occasion rather than just um . . . banging her.

In fact, after practicing sexual meditation one man, Alvin, said "Not only did the experience get me in the habit of unhurried lovemaking; afterwards I felt like I was surrounded by a feeling of calm and total connection to my partner, in contrast to being at arm's length as a result of our inability to give an inch to each other."

Compromising sexually doesn't have to mean giving up what you like on a routine basis, but being confident and open enough to mix it up will definitely bring your sex life to a deeper and more meaningful level. It's about two bodies learning to communicate and meeting halfway while "going all the way."

Chapter

WORK GETS IN OUR WAY

W ork, work, work, work, work. In today's on-the-go culture, more and more hours are being spent away from home and at the office. In fact, a survey by the National Sleep Foundation showed that the average employed American now works about 46 hours per week, with 38 percent of respondents clocking in more than 50 hours per week. As a result the NSF also reports that most adults don't get enough shuteye. We're betting that's not the only thing overworked couples aren't getting!

Not only are people spending more hours at the office than with their significant others, oftentimes the toll of such a demanding work schedule also compromises the quality of what little time a couple does get to spend together. Fatigue from long hours may zap all the energy out of a partnership, patience with each other may be strained after having to mediate with colleagues all day, and work stress may become the catalyst for relationship suicide. Add this to the simple fact that the disconnect that comes from so many hours apart can be difficult to surmount if efforts are not made to stay present in each other's lives and you see how work gets in the way of even the best-intentioned couples. But, careers and coupledom don't have to be mutually exclusive. It's okay if you have to plan out time for both in your Blackberry; the goal is staying connected, even if it requires advanced scheduling.

Work Ways and Woes

There is no doubt that work is an integral part of any partnership—the kind you do for a paycheck and the kind you invest in a relationship. And it's great if you are devoted to both, but there must be a balance or your professional and personal life will simultaneously suffer. However, professional success does not automatically doom an individual to an overworked existence with a depressing personal life. In fact, partners who both excel in the workplace can still enjoy a rich personal life in spite of their demanding jobs, but it doesn't happen without effort.

Research done at Cornell University by sociologist Phyllis Moen found that overworked couples working more than 45 hours per week reported the lowest quality of life among working couples. Couples where both partners were launching or establishing themselves in their careers also reported high degrees of stress, overload, and conflict between their work and personal life. Individuals in relationships who wished they were working less also reported a high degree of unhappiness with their situation.

However, those couples who both worked normal full-time hours (39 to 45 hours/week), but not longer, reported the highest quality of life, even higher than when one partner worked part-time. What this study indicates is that couples in "new-millennium" relationships in which both put in about the same amount of time on their jobs and neither works long hours are the ones that tend to have the highest degree of life satisfaction. Perhaps it's because they work to live, not live to work. Still, only about 24 percent of workers in dual-earner couples follow this strategy. Why is this? Well, contemporary working couples are traversing uncharted territory as they struggle to figure out the changing composition of the workforce and the division of family labor. Perhaps they underestimate what it takes to maintain a vibrant love relationship.

Even if a couple does tend towards a more traditional model where one partner works and the other stays home, there can still be situations where work gets in the way of a couple's relationship, especially if one partner is working longer than full-time hours while the other stays home to take care of their children. In fact, working couples with children at home are the most likely to have one adult—most typically the male partner—working more than forty-five hours a week, while the other partner works full-time. You can see how this scenario would leave precious little time during the week for promoting connectedness between partners. What's more, the distinction of their roles may also create a gulf between them. Pursuing a career and bringing up a child are two very different activities and unless there is good communication a couple may find themselves existing alone together.

The bottom line is that work, professional or domestic, takes up an inordinate amount of one's waking hours and may result in a couple living two separate lives while under the same roof.

Accordingly, work can get in the way of feelings of love, support, and general quality-of-life satisfaction in the personal sector. But the fact that some couples manage to work full-time and still enjoy their private life means it is possible to accomplish a healthy balance, but it might take a little more, well, work.

Sex and Work

There is no doubt that too much work can kill your sex life. Stress and fatigue don't exactly go hand-in-hand with getting it on. That is not to mention the simple fact that the more hours you spend at work, the less time you have for sex. We'd probably all have vibrant sex lives if we had no other adult responsibilities, right?

Sadly, work pressures can lead a couple to qualify for DINS (Double Income No Sex) status. Long hours can keep a couple from staying connected in several ways. Sometimes individuals will develop work crushes to help them surmount the feelings of frustration that stem from a lack of sexual connectedness with their partners at home. The problem is that this substitute for real amour often keeps individuals from trying to connect with their own romantic partner once they do get out of the office (and it is how sexual transgressions at work develop, which is never a good thing for an individual's committed nonwork relationship).

Usually "work husbands" or "work wives" serve as a source of support at the office, but partners in a relationship must make sure that their relationship with their real-life significant other doesn't suffer as a result of the attention they are paying to colleagues. It is possible to have both kinds of relationships, but parameters must be clear and priorities set.

Too much work travel can also get in the way of a healthy sex life. Time apart is always difficult for a relationship but when work takes one partner away from home more often than not, the sense of connection that comes from being a daily part of each other's lives can really start to suffer. Plus, it's physically difficult to have sex when there are miles between you and your partner, unless phone sex comes into play. Phone sex is a good option to tide you two over, but is not a permanent substitute for a real-life romp. Sexual tension can be lost when work is consistently throwing a distance wrench into the equation.

Too much stress or responsibility at work can also lead to no sex at home, or on the flip side, aberrant sex—for example, when one partner tries to reassert the lack of control they're feeling at work by getting aggressive between the sheets in order to feel in charge again. Any time sex is used in a way other than to connect with one's partner, it can damage the sexual dynamic.

While most prevailing theories in psychology hold that sex and overwork are natural enemies, the good news is that studies have shown work doesn't have to derail your sex life. One study from the University of Wisconsin-Madison found that ultimately, the daily employment grind for two-income couples actually has little effect on the frequency or quality of their sex life, but there were definitely variables within that finding that could effect a deleterious downslide for a couple's carnal time. To begin with, the real effects on the libido, according to the study, came from the amount of fatigue reported by women. However, research-ers found that both homemakers and employed women reported the same levels of fatigue, suggesting that society has a romanticized view of the homemaker's workload. Interestingly, this study showed that it's not always the number of hours worked that affects a good sex life, but rather the quality of a couple's work life. The couples that had low reports of sexual satisfaction were those that reported very low regard for their jobs. Correspondingly, if a couple is happy at work, even if long hours are banked at the office, their sex life could still hum. The lowest sex ratings of all came when men reported low job satisfaction while their female partners reported high regard for their jobs, suggesting that the combination might be tough for men to swallow since there is still a pervasive thought that they want to be the family breadwinner even in spite of changing societal roles.

The danger of attributing sexual problems exclusively to overwork is that it may allow a DINS couple to overlook deeper issues. The good news, however, is that these studies are showing it is possible to manage a career, family, and relationship without one's sex life falling apart. And, there is nothing wrong with scheduling sex either. Our society seems to place a huge amount of importance on the spontaneity of sex, but if it takes writing it into your day planner to make it happen, is that such a bad thing? Psychologists don't think so. It's about promoting a connection between two people . . . however you manage to make it happen.

Working It Out

Still worried that you and your partner are overworked and underconnected? Try adding some of the following into your routine. If at first this list seems too overwhelming with your completely overpacked agenda, start small and add in one or two items just to start. It's about re-establishing the ties-that-bind you and your partner in a positive fashion (i.e., the last thing we want to do is add any more stress to your already pressure-filled lives). That said, the following will definitely help bring you close even when work is dragging you in opposite directions.

Make Contact During the Day

It may be brief, but touching base during a busy workday conveys a delightful reminder of the importance with which you regard the relationship. You are taking a thoughtful moment out of your day to say, in effect, "thinking of you." And, of course, if your partner contacts you, unless you are dealing with something very urgent, or are in the middle of a high-level meeting, take the call or respond to an e-mail promptly. This makes an important statement to your partner as to the priority of your relationship.

Don't Bring Work Home

Walking through the door with the Bluetooth stuck on your ear and the Blackberry engaged in your hand is not inviting. Especially if you work long hours, when you are home, be present in the moment. It is often not the long hours that degrade a relationship (unless the hours are extraordinary, like 100-hour workweeks), but the lack of quality time when home. Consistent with the quality time issue, don't rely heavily on the television. Sharing the same couch silently is not a model of togetherness.

Bring Conversation about Work Home

Many couples make the mistake of "I don't want to live through my day again." This is a mistake. Think about it: You may work ten hours a day (including commute time), and sleep about seven hours. If you eliminate discussion of your work life, you have chosen to reduce the common ground between you and your partner drastically. Instead, make your partner part of your work life by discussing those aspects of your day that he is most interested in.

Be Receptive to Career Talk

Of course, the listening partner is advised to be receptive. Making one partner's work (or each other's career, if both are employed) part of each other's lives is a good thing. Much better than viewing the career (one or both) as an enemy or competitor. Asking questions and showing interest is bonding since it expresses an attention to something important to your partner. After all, she spends the majority of her waking hours at work.

Come Home Early One Night

Despite a heavy schedule it is wise to connect face to face for some quality time midweek. Coming home early doesn't mean cutting out after lunch. Simply leaving work an hour or so before the typical quitting time is sufficient. If affordable, going out for a light dinner, leaving the usual at-home distractions behind, is a good idea. Lots of couples find that this works well for them, even if they stay later on other evenings to make up the time. Bear in mind that real quality time can go a long way toward bridging the contact gap in busy schedules.

Get the Kids to Sleep

If there are children in the picture, while it is usually a good idea to be flexible with the rules of the household, the sleep routine will better serve all involved if there is a strict adherence policy. Yes, the children want and need their "pound of parental flesh" attention from their parents, but that works best if it is intense and (mostly) exclusive in the earlier part of the evening while later in the evening, before exhaustion sets in, is reserved for the adults.

Practice the Art of Brief, Personal Sharing

Exchanging personal thoughts, especially for people who can get caught up too easily in the business of the day, is critical. This doesn't take a lot of time; it is more a factor of being attuned to your own and your partner's feelings. For example, a man or woman may be getting dressed in the morning and say something like, "You know, I'm really anxious about the meeting today. I hope it goes well because it is important for my career, and for us." Two sentences that take under ten seconds that convey a lot. These intimate exchanges where partners briefly share their feelings and take each other into their thoughts, concerns, and aspirations, can make the difference between a truly romantic relationship and a relationship that is more like a business partnership.

Plan Weekends

Make a plan during the week that will allow for quality time spent together when work is out of the picture. This may be just making reservations at a favorite restaurant ahead of time so you two can look forward to that meal all week, or something more elaborate such as the occasional out-of-town escape. Whatever, the idea is to make togetherness a priority and schedule it just like you would work-time obligations Monday through Friday.

If there are children in your life, seek out activities that are kid-friendly so that there is a nice balance between interacting with the children and interacting with each other. Going to a park, for example, so that the kids can play with other kids, and intermittently interact with you, provides time for the children and time for each other. In contrast, going someplace that will not engage the children is going to be exclusively child-centered and will not provide opportunity for adult bonding with each other.

Protect Your Time

For busy people it is very important to avoid getting caught up in or volunteering for noncritical activities. A relationship takes a degree of tending if it is to be viable and vibrant. Consequently, it is unwise to be too generous with giving away time that could be shared with your partner. Often, this amounts to being assertive and maintaining priorities so that your tight schedule is not unnecessarily stressed. For example, do you really have to say "yes" to your friend's request to help her son write his college essay? Prioritize your relationship over extraneous time zappers.

Plan Vacations

Even with tight budgets, a getaway is often possible, and may even be vital. If it can't be a luxury hotel, it can be a drive-to getaway at a modest bed and breakfast. Sometimes even an overnight change of scenery can boost a relationship sagging from too much sameness. Consider it this way: Your relationship has an account, similar to a bank account. There are deposits and withdrawals. Meeting a work deadline while working endless hours is a withdrawal; a getaway, even brief, is a deposit since it adds to the overall feeling of goodwill between love partners.

Even with all of these steps in place, it can still be tough to maintain a sense of sexual intimacy with your partner when time demands and sometimes distance keeps you from hitting the sheets regularly. So how can you strengthen your connection carnally as well as emotionally while separated? Read on for some physical connectors.

Sexual Solution

You're away from home too much of the time. When you're home you're tired, busy, stressed, or preoccupied. The connection with your partner is suffering. You need a relationship boost, and it needs to be something that will bring a smile to your face when you think about each other in the midst of a typically busy day.

Memorable sex is just the thing to revitalize and restore the connection. Sex isn't depleting, it's energizing, especially if it's quick, easy, and provocative. We're talking quickies here, but not the wham-bam, thank-you-ma'am quickie of old. Occasional quickie sex, primal, spontaneous—or planned, with mischief, in forbidden locations—where both he and she get rocked, is just what's needed to bring back the connection that has withered.

These quickies are provocative encounters that may not always be quick, but are always different; they break the usual pattern, bring in elements of daring and the forbidden that are not part of typical lovemaking. A quickie may not always be speedy, but it should get your blood flowing and intensify your connection.

The point is that a no-holds-barred, rip-off-each-other's-clothes-with-your-teeth-right-here-right-now sex is not only the best way to have more fun in bed, it's also a way to keep a busy relationship from feeling like—dare we say it—a tolerable, but dispassionate habit. The new form of quickie is better than a double espresso and you'll both find yourselves thinking of the other a lot more.

THE QUICKIE

Here are some beginning quickie scenarios. Remember, they may not always be quick (although any of our suggestions can be abbreviated), but they're different.

Each of these variations brings a touch of variety and a bit of the less conventional to break into the routine of your pattern of being sexual.

Like spices in cooking, some people respond to a hint and others need a large dollop before they experience a new sensation. We're beginning with a hint; in the "recipes" to come we'll ramp up the spice.

Try any or all of these and watch your sex life soar no matter what's going on in your work life (there's always time for a quickie).

Step 1

Try an A.M. stimulation session. Each morning, before the two of you get up, spend just a couple of the minutes getting each other stimulated. Orgasm is not the point. It's about the tease; it is about creating something to take with you in your mind's eye through the day.

Step 2

Think outside the bed. Have sex somewhere you might not usually have it, but in your own place. Try some of the following locations:

♂♀ *Shower.* Great for oral sex. The water gently trickling over the head and shoulders of the partner kneeling at the other's genitals adds to the pleasure.

♂♀ *Living room.* You can have sex sitting in a chair, on the sofa, the floor, maybe the coffee table. A fireplace in winter adds ambiance, and candlelight works too.

♂♀ *Kitchen.* Floor, table, counters. If the man is tall, try having intercourse with the female sitting on the counter while he stands.

♂♀ *Dining room.* Chairs, table, floor. The association with food can make sex more interesting, especially if the table hasn't been cleared.

♂♀ *Garage.* Have you ever made love on the hood of a parked car? Make sure the hood isn't hot and you don't have one of those motion sensitive alarms! Look around the garage for other ideas. Improvise.

Step 3

Arrive early, come later. Get somewhere ten minutes early. Stay in the car and stimulate each other for ten minutes only. Don't be late.

Step 4

Try mouthing off! Surprise each other with a few minutes of oral sex. This can be for one of you this time and the other next time.

Step 5

Be a flasher. Tease your partner. You're dressed, running ten minutes late, hurrying out the door. Your partner is still getting dressed or lingering over breakfast. On your way out, flash him or her. Yes, flash. Quickly expose your breast, hike your skirt to show some leg, pull something out of your pants. Then exit, leaving your partner with a terrific visual to carry around all day (and wanting more).

Step 6

Stay dressed. Don't take your clothes off. Remember when you and your significant other first got involved? That primal, animalistic groping? Remember being so desperate for your lover's body that you didn't take the time to remove clothing, only pushed aside the necessary items? Start kissing on the sofa (or in the car) and recapture the feelings.

Step 7

Combine food and sex. Even adults like to play with their food occasionally. Take food to bed with you and feed each other. Get more creative than that. For example, melt some chocolate and apply it liberally to each other's body and lick it off (bonus: chocolate is not only delicious, it contains phenylethylamine, a mood-boosting chemical that can incite lust).

Step 8

Paint your bodies. Use water-soluble fingerpaints or bodypaints— some come flavored—to decorate one another's nude bodies. Paint yourself to look like the members of primitive tribes and make love the way you imagine they do.

Tech Sex

WHILE phone sex is very titillating because the voice is a powerful turn-on tool, technology today has made it possible for even more varied sexually charged exchanges while separated. Take advantage of these and pretty soon you may be saying "Tech please."

♂ **Text messaging.** "Text me" is now part of our cultural vocabulary. This easy way of sending quick messages via phone is also a superb sexual tool. You may not be able to call your partner several times a day, but a well-timed "What are you wearing?" or "Can't wait to take off your work clothes" can go a long way towards building sexual excitement.

♀ **Camera phone.** Imagine your partner's grin when her phone beeps with a new photo message and she opens the phone file to see a picture of you half-dressed or perhaps a shot of you with your favorite sex toy. The possibilities are endless.

♀ **Instant messaging.** Yahoo, AOL, and many other online services offer versions of Instant Messaging software that allow you to chat online with your partner. Conversations can get very flirty on these services, so be sure you're using a personal computer!

♀ **Chat room.** Did you know you can still set up a private chat room online? Unexpectedly invite your partner to a chat room during the day. You can even both take on fake names and have a good time being "suggestive" under your assumed personas.

♀ **Webcam.** With a webcam attachment, you can actually see each other while you chat online. This is an especially great feature if you travel a great deal. Check out services like Skype.com, which allow you to talk through your computer while engaging in video streaming (rates are surprisingly reasonable). It's almost like being together in person (and you can definitely take something off while talking/watching on the computer). It's like phone sex plus visuals.

Chapter 9

WE DON'T HANDLE
CHANGE WELL

L ife is a journey. Nothing stays the same, even if you want it
to. Times change, locations change, careers change, families
change, the weather changes, you change. And yes, relationships
change.

But even with all the constant flux surrounding us on a daily
basis, people can be surprisingly resistant. Maybe it's a fear of the
unknown, maybe it's a desire to maintain a comfortable existence,
maybe it's an urge to find stability, or all of the above, but even
within the context of trying to prevent something from shifting,
there will still be change. It's an inevitability, but the way you
handle it is what will ultimately determine its effect.

Perhaps the most mutable obstacle course in life is the one
connected to your relationships. From the time you begin to
share in the sandbox through adulthood, you learn and grow as
a result of your interaction with others. It informs, it teaches, and
ultimately with each relationship you undertake it changes you a
bit, whether you're aware of it or not.

Life presents a series of hoops for you to jump through and climbing walls for you to scale. The trick is to figure out who is on your team along the way that can help you get through these challenges. And hopefully, your partner is the person you will count on most as an adult to help you surmount the curve balls thrown your way.

Unfortunately sometimes a couple will cruise along in a happy relationship until faced with a change and at that moment, instead of turning to each other, things start to fracture. Change may require a rethinking of the parameters of your togetherness, and for some couples that ends up causing a "disconnect" instead of bringing them closer because they were mentally unprepared for any shifts in their relationship. Preferences change so that old rituals fade, career demands interfere with traditional time together, and if a child joins the relationship, it's a whole new deal. Still, many couples find themselves trying to keep things perfectly status quo in their relationships. It's the one area they want to control.

However, keeping your relationship exactly the same is impossible. If you want to survive as a duo, you're going to have to learn how to adjust to the changes thrown your way as well. Flexibility is vital to any sustainable long-term relationship.

The Relationship Cycle

Just as one's life goes through phases, so too does one's relationships. Partners in a long-term arrangement can expect the beginning of their affair to be a time filled with lots of pleasurable activities and minimal sacrifice. At this point the decisions made are where to dine and what movie to see, not heavier things like making joint financial decisions and apportioning household responsibilities. Spontaneity is high, as is the novelty of their companionable and sexual activity.

Once the honeymoon period is suddenly replaced by responsibility and decreased freedom as a couple butts up against real-life decisions, many couples don't survive. It's the make-or-break point when you learn if you're both willing to give enough to make something work and to keep moving forward while dealing with the changes that are happening in your relationship. Gone are the days of no emotional entanglements as you happily skipped through a state of oxytocin-induced love bliss. When real-life hits, it's a change to a new, more challenging phase in your relationship. And it's sink or swim. You either discover a way to deal with change effectively as a duo or you will start to see cracks in the foundation you attempted to build during the early phase of your togetherness.

It is at this point that your roles may have to be renegotiated a bit. Desire for personal and career satisfactions has to be integrated with the changes that come from being part of a committed couple. The "oneness" and romance that were characteristic of the courtship period have altered, and now you'll have to start working others into the equation as well (e.g., friends, some of whom may not be mutually esteemed; families, including a controlling parent, or perhaps two; and so on). Lovers do not exist in a vacuum and eventually that will include interactions and other platonic relationships coming into your partnership. But all of these will include changes for your dynamic as a duo as well.

Alterations in your dynamic will be further heightened if you continue a typical relationship trajectory and eventually find yourselves married, having children, raising a family, readjusting when the kids leave home, and eventually dealing with the reconnection that is necessary during retirement. You can see how much change factors into each of these cycles and how even in this very brief and admittedly quite incomplete sketch, it is evident that relationships are constantly evolving. Each new stage brings with it hurdles to overcome. In fact, studies have even shown this to be true time and again. For example:

♂ Parents of young children show a substantial drop in the amount of time they spend conversing with each other and a similar decline in social activities.

♀ Couple interests and activities tend to taper as either the man or woman (or both) are promoted to more responsible job levels.

♂ Arguments over money tend to increase as a family's income increases.

♀ Sexual infidelity is more likely to occur when a man or woman reaches the late-middle years (ironically, this could be the time when people start looking for some change as a result of resisting it).

None of these findings definitively doom long-term relationships—change is not the enemy—but the manner in which it is approached will absolutely determine if it will make or break a relationship. Indeed, a formidable barrier to growth and prosperity as a couple is an unwillingness to adapt to changing conditions. Let us reiterate, however, that not only is change inevitable, it is also *necessary* when situations alter.

Resisting Versus Embracing

When face to face with change, there are really two options: resisting or embracing. If the former is chosen, there is probably an element of fear in the mix. If the latter path is taken, acceptance and flexibility come into play.

Because change is frequently correlated with temporary instability as roles or situations are reassessed, many people find themselves inherently resistant to change on a regular basis. In fact, frequently the dominating barrier to relational satisfaction is resistance to change—whether it is in relationships with colleagues, employees, friends, family members, or lovers. This is applicable not only when faced with circumstantial change but also when an individual is asked to make personal changes for the sake of the relationship. Consider this scene in a couple therapist's office. He: How can you say you want a divorce, I'm the same guy you fell in love with fifteen years ago, I haven't changed! She: That's why. Exactly!

In a wonderful example of paradox, however, most of the time people will only change if they feel that they don't have to! If a resistant individual feels himself being pushed towards altering something about himself (be it to change personal habits or some relationship mannerism), there is a high probability that he'll not only fight the change, but possibly even swing in the opposite direction of the request. Think of it as a mini-mutation rebellion. It may manifest in a variety of forms—perhaps lack of cooperation, intentional mood-triggering, substance abuse, or even infidelity (which is the ultimate rebellion since, if discovered, it will seriously damage or end the primary relationship).

The bottom line is that everyone struggles to maintain their unique identity, so when faced with the prospect of having to change some aspect of ourselves for another, it immediately sends off a warning signal in our brains (even if the requested change might be a good thing for us or the relationship). Most people are naturally opposed to change because of the insecurity that comes along with it and most of us resist, covertly or blatantly, the demand that we live up to others' visions of what we "should" be. What's more, for many the request for change is received as "You are not good enough as you are." For this reason, a key factor in presenting a request for change often involves reframing a message so that "ego" doesn't get in the way, which may also mean making some changes in how you view the situation.

In order to be more open to change, we must learn to accept that change is going to happen and find ways to deal with change that are not accusatory but rather accepting. It's not only about realizing that shift happens, but also being able to recognize that we have the power to alter our own viewpoint in relation to an event. We can get upset, or we can try to "reframe" things and move forward which will give a situation new meaning and minimize the fear that goes along with change.

It is certainly a desirable wish to want life to proceed smoothly while people act fairly and thoughtfully towards each other. Wishing is one thing, but *demands* for utopia are unrealistic in real life. It is simply not how the world operates and therefore the insistence that things must proceed in a perfect way leads to emotional upset and self-defeating behaviors.

According to the principle of reframing, instead of being carried along feeling utterly powerless and out of control, we must accept some responsibility for our own fate; it is a personal choice to resist or embrace change. You can make a decision whether you will let something lead you to a state of serious distress, or you can embrace that you're going through a fluctuation and try to find a positive way to confront your fears and deal effectively with whatever challenge is in front of you.

When faced with change, try asking yourself: "How can I view this situation in the most productive and realistic manner possible?" The result will likely be that you can replace the panicked feeling that things are moving too quickly around you with a sense of calm that you can handle the situation, restore harmony, and avoid unnecessary stress in the process.

The thing that dictates behavior is our own unique perceptions of ourselves and the world in which we live, plus the meaning we give to the events of our lives. This fact seems obvious enough, but in reality, most of us do not appreciate the enormity of its application. The point here is this: All behavior is open to many interpretations, and the particular interpretation chosen is crucial to the feelings and behavioral reactions that are generated at any given time. It's resist or embrace. But the more open you allow yourself to be when accepting the changes you face daily, the easier it will become.

Sex and Change

As we've already established, change sometimes makes people feel temporarily insecure. For many couples, add sex to the change mix, stir, and the resulting cocktail is, well, super potent. While pleasurable, of course, who doesn't have that "Am I good enough?" or "Is my body hot enough?" panic moment while getting intimate? Therefore, asking for change in the bedroom where a person may already feel slightly insecure . . . well, you can see how jockeying for a shift in your sexual behavior as a couple can become a slippery slope.

Sex tends to make people feel vulnerable because intimacy can bring a couple closer (assuming of course that there is some emotional connection during the act). Add the insecurity that comes with change to the vulnerability already inherent in sexual interaction and it obviously becomes a tenuous negotiation when one partner desires alterations between the sheets. No one wants to add pressure to their sex life. It's supposed to be a release and a bonding experience, a time to bathe in the moment. But, if one partner isn't satisfied, there will have to be some degree of change in order for the relationship to survive long term as dissatisfaction can precipitate the death of one's sex life, which clearly does nothing to help sustain a relationship. Communication is vital and that requires openness to change and exploration for both partners. It's about working together, yet again—finding your way to a solution that incorporates change without rocking the boat—but hopefully rockin' the bed.

The other way that change will undoubtedly affect your sex life is when change outside the bedroom is not dealt with effectively. As we've noted, anything that happens to your dynamic as a couple may shift your between-the-sheets dynamic as well. Consequently, the result of resistance to change anywhere is likely to be a sex life that is suffering from the effects of the tumult and resentment.

Also keep in mind that change need not be discordant for it still to have great influence on your sex life. For example, the addition of children to the equation. A couple may find they have less energy, time, or interest in sex as a result of the responsibilities and life changes that come along with child rearing. On the surface some people might say "Well, that's to be expected," when they can't recall the last intimate pairing. However, we would like to point out that a relationship deprived of physical intimacy isn't the most positive adaptation to change.

Basically, negotiating sex and change (be it situational or carnal) is about achieving balance. It's recognizing that everything in life goes in waves—periods of contact and periods of withdrawal—and your sex life is no different. But if you allow change to alter your sex life to the point of indifference or nonexistence, then you are going to see the effects trickle out of the bedroom as well. While it's not the entire basis for a relationship, sex is an integral part of it and you must keep that element vital if you hope to maintain your connection as a couple. That very connectedness is what will allow you to weather any change together.

Becoming a Change-ling

Change is difficult, especially if there is work involved to make it happen effectively. In order to institute changes in some area of your relationship, try following these guidelines as they will help you get where you need to go as a couple without letting the prospect of change throw your duo into a state of upheaval.

Be Gradual

Attempt to effect change in a manner that is too sweeping and you will likely fail. The same thing goes for trying to alter a relationship too quickly or too greatly in too short a period of time, which may lead to feelings of disillusionment and despair. A better bet? Instead of making requests for an all-at-once overhaul, which may be overwhelming, consider making them gradually and successively. This will help take some of the fear of change out of the equation since it will happen incrementally, making it less perceptible.

Be Ready for Resistance

Change is hard. You will do better if you go in accepting a certain degree of resistance from the outset. Further compounding the difficulty we all have with the change process is the fact that change in relationships involves the risk of getting closer to one's significant other. Remember that while we crave the rewards of closeness, many of us fear the increased vulnerability and possibility of hurt that accompany intimacy. That may also manifest as resistance, but the good news is it may be surmounted if the bond is strong and there is still forward movement happening in the relationship.

Be Persistent

If at first you don't succeed, keep at it. It's not unreasonable to expect that both you and your significant other will occasionally test the sincerity of each other's change efforts. Testing may take the form of provocation ("You don't really want anything to change, do you?"), questioning of motivation ("You're doing this only because you think I'll cheat on you if you don't"), expressing feelings of hopelessness ("These changes are superficial and are not going to truly fix anything"), and/or a return to earlier behaviors ("I wish it were June again when we were happy"). By viewing testing as a normal part of the change process and continuing with the restorative behavior despite temporary discouragement, you can set a new precedent. Don't panic, persevere.

Be Positive

It's much easier to build up than break down. Therefore, keep in mind that you'll be more effective if you accentuate the positive rather than try to directly eliminate the negative. For example, rather than asking a partner to not be as critical, the desired response might be more effectively gained if you asked her to make an effort to increase positive, appreciative comments. Undesirable behavior is more effectively controlled when confronted in this manner. Asking someone to straight-up stop doing something is likely to send resistance flags flying. On the flip side, asking for a positive change makes it seem less like an attack is being waged and more like a simple request is being made.

Be Action-Oriented

Actions speak louder than words. You've heard the phrase, but it really rings true here. Although feelings and beliefs are critically important to the ability to survive change as a couple, neither carries the impact reserved for action. Verbalizing your love to your partner does not have the same degree of potency as a demonstration. It is what you do rather than what you profess that will ultimately make the difference.

Once you start to deal with change more effectively outside of the bedroom (or even whilst working to incorporate these change-makers into your repertoire as a couple), you can start to seal the deal with some physical manifestations as well. Because change can happen on many levels, you might as well start incorporating your whole being into the flux that is life.

Sexual Solution

Do you have some issues you need to reframe or some changes you need to accommodate in your relationship? Of course you do; we all do. To make the integration more complete, it's a great idea to add a physical element to your reframing experience in an attempt to solidify and memorialize your efforts. In other words, it might be time for your relationship to undergo a sex change. Think of it this way: If you've conquered change in the bedroom, change elsewhere in your relationship is going to be a snap. Okay, maybe not a snap, but easier.

STRETCHING SEXUALLY

When change-resistance has frozen relationship growth, there is a likelihood that both partners stretching their comfort zone is minimal or nonexistent. The danger is a stale sex life, which can be the kiss of death in a long-term relationship. Exploring change in the bedroom and carrying a new attitude over the threshold is an excellent and potent counter.

The goal is to stretch your sexual repertoire a bit and bring the relationship to a new level. The experience is about small, simple moves that make a big impact. Nothing makes the bedroom buzz with erotic electricity like debuting a new sexual scenario you've been thinking about, especially if you think it's naughty. And nothing carries the excitement of change like the memories of sexual adventure brought on by novelty.

Spontaneously suggesting something different on any given day has the potential to elevate a same-old, same-old pleasure session into a heart-pounding, fasten-your-seat-belt romp. And once you have your hearts racing with a bold initiative, change will likely be transformed from something to avoid into a challenge to relish.

Is there a downside? Of course. You are going to lose your inhibitions. Try any or all of these naughty "sexgestions" for a change in your bedroom routine. First change? Take off your clothes. Then get busy mixing it up!

Step 1

Do an about-face. Instead of the standard woman-on-top position, try turning it around so the female partner faces his legs instead of his torso. The guy gets a great view of his gal from behind, including her behind, and the slightly different angle will make the sex feel new and exciting for both partners. What's more, not facing him may give the woman more freedom to feel naughty. Of course, you can always arrange things so that both of you can view the action in the mirror as well. The idea is to take a sex position that you usually perform one way and turn it on its head (or side or back or whatever the case may be).

Step 2

Role-play. If you find it exciting watching yourself, you may find it even steamier watching someone else—that is, both of you pretending to be someone else. What fantasy of yours is recurring? Suggest a little method acting—each of you playing the characters from a recurring fantasy. It can be the desperate housewife who meets the electrician, or the librarian who takes off her glasses, opens her blouse, and cuts loose. Role-playing gives you the freedom to step out of yourself and say or do things the "real you" wouldn't normally do. Plus, rehearsing for your performance is hot in itself.

Step 3

Get wet. There are days that you rush through the shower faster than it takes to watch the morning weather report. And there are days when time is not of the essence. On one of those more leisurely mornings concentrate on how good the soapy lather feels as you work your hands all over your wet body. For example, if the female is initiating this, she can caress her breasts, and slowly work down to her inner thighs, eventually moving to her hot zone. Feeling warmed up, she calls out to her guy and tells him to bring in a towel. When he sees the expression on her face and the mischief in her eyes, he'll get the message (and probably be soapy and wet himself before he knows it). Feel free to mix up who starts this move, but make sure the end result is some good clean—or not so clean—fun.

Step 4

Heat up the heat. This move is about mixing up sensations. You can certainly explore many variations, such as using mints or other stimulants to add new pleasure dimensions. In this variation, however, we'll give an example where the female partner initiates a change in stimulus by adding heat to her guy's body and boosting his sensitivity. To begin, she should put a warm cup of water by the bed and take a sip to get her mouth warmed up before going down on him. After swallowing the warm water, she should take another small sip, but this time hold it in her mouth as she takes him back into her mouth as well. Swishing the water around his penis for a few seconds before swallowing again will give a whole new whirlpool sensation for the guy who will probably feel like he's gone to BJ heaven. Women are similarly responsive to changes in temperature or sensation so feel free to make sure this change goes both ways.

Step 5

Move out of the bedroom. Whether it's a spontaneous romp on the kitchen counter or some action in the parking lot before a dinner out, exploring a bit of exhibitionism could be in order. The possibility of getting caught is a huge turn-on. There's intense excitement in the idea of being a little bad. One move to try? Encourage your partner to slip her hand between your legs and slyly start rubbing your genitals while watching a movie (make it a scary movie and your libido will already be heightened since sex and fear tend to travel the same neurological pathways to the brain). Too much of a risk? When your partner is least expecting it, stick your hand into his or her pant pocket saying that you're looking for change (don't wait for permission, just start groping for um . . . quarters). Then give your partner a slight genital massage until you can feel arousal starting to happen. At that point, whisper a promise for "later" in his or her ear. The result will be a "privates" moment in public that is very, very hot.

Step 6

Strip each other. Set yourselves up in front of a full-length mirror so you can see the show. Both of you, one at a time, are going to pull a classic steamy movie-scene move on each other. Begin to peel off your partner's clothing one piece at a time, slowly and seductively. Strip everything but underwear to create a monster tease. Then, up the ante by taking off the underwear slowly and seductively with your mouth as you nibble, suck, and lick those sensitive genital areas. This whole scene is heightened by the fact you can watch your partner and yourself (and vice versa) in the mirror. Sexy, sexy, sexy. Now, switch until you both end up naked and primed for sex.

Step 7

Try a simultaneous self-strip. First, watch a film of a professional stripper in the act to get some tips. Then spend some time practicing on your own (without your partner watching). It'll make you feel sexy and naughty, the perfect attitude for the adaptation to change. After a few undress rehearsals, get ready to strip at the same time for each other, but keep a distance so that each partner can look but not touch. Viewing the strip, especially if it is done with a lustful gleam, will spike his testosterone and fuel a craving to go further. In the final act before the grand finale, touch yourselves teasingly. For the grand finale back into the nearest wall, and take a deep breath, because you will be up against each other before you exhale.

Step 8

Make a 911 sex call. Dial your partner just around quitting time and in the earthiest tone possible tell him or her that you're home already, you're naked and you're ready and waiting for him or her to get off— work that is—so you can start your own private happy hour. The idea that you're feeling like an animal in heat and calling to make a "take-in" order will have a primal impact on your partner. There's nothing like feeling desired to create desire. Make sure you're still naked when your partner walks in the door.

Step 9

Aural sex. If you listen carefully, there are sounds in your house, some from the outdoors and some from the hum of appliances. It is time to add your own sounds, the sounds of your lovemaking ringing through the air. Your lovemaking will be sensitized and heightened when you add sound to it, since nearly all of us are aroused by the sounds we make and hear during sex. Groans, sighs, moans, whis- pers, cries—sex has a language of its own.

Sometimes we hold back expressions of pleasure during sex due to embarrassment or inhibition. If you're having silent or barely audible sex, consider bringing some more change into your sex life by turning up the sound and the excitement at the same time. Take some deep breaths, picture yourself in a sultry mood, and let your body totally relax. Then experiment with sounds you could utter the next time you're in the sack. The key is to determine what you feel good doing and work from there. If you're apprehensive, start with heavy breathing, which in itself can make sex more mind-blowing.

Chapter

10

WE'RE REELING
FROM AN AFFAIR

I s monogamy possible? It's becoming a very real question in this day and age and one that is getting a lot of debate from both men and women. In the past, most couples would have answered an unequivocal "yes" but today things are a little more well, shades of gray.

With the advent of the Internet, infidelity can be arranged with the click of a button. It's so easy to stray that individual resolve and commitment to being in a couple must be strong or the temptation can prove to be overwhelming for some individuals.

Additionally, sex is no longer a taboo subject. With shows like *Sex and the City* and even HBO's practically soft-porn *Tell Me You Love Me* showcasing sex, infidelity, and relationship dysfunction on television on a daily basis, people are recognizing that what was once not even discussed is now a reality of modern life.

Unfortunately, what this also illustrates is that the choice to remain monogamous is becoming more difficult in more relationships all the time. It is not uncommon at all for men and women to act out the deficiencies of their relationship through an affair. But there are always ramifications and fallout from these behaviors and transgressions.

What it comes down to is that affairs are major betrayals, which once revealed have very strong consequences . . . sexually and otherwise.

The Clandestine Coverup

Affairs wreak havoc on relationships. There is no tiptoeing around this fact. They're not called "relationship wreckers" for nothing. By definition, an affair—be it of the heart, the body, or both—is something that happens in a fashion that is extracurricular to the purported primary relationship. The result of this "outside" influence is sometimes overt, like more time spent away from the primary relationship and sometimes covert, as in a subtle distancing from the primary relationship, but always deleterious to the bond that should be holding a partnership together.

In fact, that is a large part of the problem; affairs don't lend themselves to sharing and openness. But you need a certain degree of divulgence to promote long-term viability in a relationship. As soon as the secret-keeping starts, the door to a truly open, reciprocally giving relationship slams shut. Hiding an affair is the ultimate lie and in turn, leads to more lying. It causes the person involved to operate in a cautious manner in their primary relationship—and sometimes with others as well, since part of their life is secret.

What this does is throw up new walls to intimacy. All that time two people spent getting to know each other is now deconstructed piece by piece. How many times have you heard someone facing the disappointment of an affair in their relationship say, "It's like I don't even know who my partner is anymore . . . and I now wonder if I ever did." An affair may not seem like it would change the personalities of the players involved in the primary relationship, but it will. Suddenly the adulterous partner becomes more secretive or possibly even paranoid since he is carrying around a huge secret all day and the cheated-on partner may start feeling more needy or moody and not even be sure from whence the feelings stem. The result of this is a shift in the duo's dynamic. And it's not a shift towards more connectedness with each other. Indeed, the rule of secrets is simple: Those sharing the secret are drawn closer to each other and those from whom the secret is kept are distanced.

In addition to the guardedness, deception, and lying that are an integral part of an affair, there is usually a corresponding change in attitude and behavior within the relationship that also may arouse a mate's suspicions. Some affairs involve the cheating partner stepping back from his mate, playing out a loyalty to his lover. Other times, the offender becomes more amorous in an effort to compensate for her external "playing" (oftentimes in an effort to convince herself that what she's doing isn't *that* bad, thus protecting her own sense of what's right and wrong). Still others behave in a way that's simply uncharacteristic of their usual mannerisms such that they inadvertently break down whatever emotional safety still existed in the primary relationship.

Oftentimes, there is a marked individual change that goes along with an affair as well. For example, the adulterous partner may think they're concealing their amorous toying, but may inadvertently give away the infidelity just by subtle changes in their own behavior. It may be barely perceptible to the outside world, but within the context of the relationship, it may be noticeable to the cheated-on partner. Usually couples have a way of relating to each other and when another person is thrown into the mix (covertly via the affair), sometimes that interaction may shift just enough that things start to feel "off" in the primary relationship. And it may not always be in the stereotypical ways you would expect (i.e., one partner pulling away or becoming less affectionate). Whatever the tipoff, however, once there start to be shifts in a couple's dynamic as a result of extracurricular dalliances, things get more difficult to sustain. And the more involved the outside relationship, the greater the risk the adulterous party takes since in that case, there will likely be more noticeable (as opposed to subtle) changes in behavior and attitude.

Typically, at this juncture the cheating partner will begin to escalate the lying: "Oh, I think I must be letting work get to me," or "I'm just exhausted, I need a break." If his mate does not buy these veiled answers, and suspicion continues to be aroused, the lying balloons, the secret expands, and the trust continues to deflate.

When Affair Signs Surface

While some affairs may go undiscovered for a lifetime, that's probably not the norm and they're probably not truly undetected: There may be signs that are consciously or subconsciously being ignored in an effort to protect the relationship. And the reasons for affairs are not always just that the attraction to another person was too great to be controlled. Oftentimes, there are a myriad of other reasons that prompted the betrayal that had little or nothing to do with temptation!

On that note, while sexual betrayal itself is bad enough—a nuclear assault on the noninvolved partner—sometimes the most serious breach may be an affair laced with an unconscious intent or message. For example, cheating could be an attempt to force the hand of a mate who refuses to acknowledge that the relationship is in trouble. Thus, in an empty relationship, a mate may flaunt infidelity to provoke a breakup—it becomes a "secret" weapon if you will. In this case, it's a way to get the other person to dissolve the union so the adulterer doesn't have to. This is a totally passive-aggressive way to get out and not the most adult choice but unfortunately it happens more than it should.

When a relationship is merely troubled, an affair that is left open to discovery may be a signal from the affair-involved partner to pay more attention to the relationship. It may be a wakeup call for all sorts of issues, but it definitely speaks to one very loudly, "Look at me, look at me! I'm sexy!" Of course, most people do not willingly acknowledge that the brazenness of their sexual involvement conveys such purposes.

Nor is the intended effect typically achieved. A man who is indiscreetly conducting an affair may be doing so in order to punish his partner for past upsets but instead of responding with remorse, his partner may retaliate with hostility or perhaps even with an affair of her own (i.e., "Hurt me and I'll hurt you right back"). Or a woman who thinks having an affair will help encourage her primary partner to be more attentive may find herself alone when he walks out on her. In some cases the hurt partner may be completely devastated and react very strongly, perhaps violently, or attempt to harm himself. In other words, playing with infidelity is like playing with fire.

That said, sometimes an individual will deny a mate's obvious affair involvement because acknowledgment may be so threatening to her sense of emotional security that it cannot be tolerated. Thus, the noninvolved and the involved partner enter into a conspiracy to cover up the clandestine. In fact, a fair number of men and women employ the denial defense. Rather than confront the truth, they unconsciously join in the secret and establish a pseudo-relationship, wherein the satisfaction derived from outside activities masks the emptiness within. Extravagant entertaining, shopping ventures, frequent traveling, elaborate redecorating/renovations, and job-hopping can be attempts to fill a relationship void (or hide their complicit cheating/truth-dodging dynamic). But beyond the surface where everything looks "fine" to the untrained eye, keep in mind that things are not okay in this type of situation. It will eat away at the individual suppressing the knowledge of the transgression and the relationship simultaneously.

Whatever the coping mechanism or avoidance tactic, the bottom line is that an affair is not likely to strengthen a primary relationship. Discovered or undiscovered, detected or undetected . . . the result of an affair will most likely be heartache.

Sex and Affairs

This one may seem obvious since sex is what gets a couple into this predicament in the first place. But beyond the sexual transgressions outside of a couple's relationship, there are other ways that sex may be used, abused, and confused before, during, and after an affair.

To begin with, sex (or lack thereof) in the primary relationship may serve as an indicator that there is a rift. Once the concept of monogamy implicit in a coupled relationship is breached, there will be obvious fractures in a couple's intimacy, even if the affair is still covert. It is not possible for one person to be cheating (or even thinking about cheating) and not have this action/thought process surface somehow.

The adulterous partner may think she is doing a superb job of hiding the infidelity, but sometimes it is the littlest things that give it away. Perhaps it is a change in position (i.e., you always used to "do it" facing each other so you could kiss, but now, for example, suddenly one partner prefers doggie style since there is less emotional connection that way). This could indicate that one partner is pulling away from the relationship, or that his mind is elsewhere (or on someone else). Or it could be more obvious like diminished frequency. Sometimes it is more subtle—call it intuition if you will. Because lovers get so close during the act of lovemaking, they can also feel when something is awry. It's a sixth sense that the connectedness that was once felt is somehow hindered.

Obviously, any of these manifestations will affect the sex life of a couple where cheating is being considered or has already started. It will lead to less sync in and out of bed. It may also lead to feelings of confusion, such as "We used to be so close and our lovemaking was so connected, but now I'm left feeling cold after intimacy. What happened?" This is especially true for nonaffair-involved partners. Chances are they will feel a change sexually before they ever even know the extent of what is or has been going on outside their relationship.

Once an affair is revealed, you can probably surmise that it's usually the death of a couple's sex life as they've known it—at least at the present time. It's virtually impossible for the aggrieved partner to entertain thoughts of intimacy for a while after discovering the person he thought was his, was actually someone else's as well! Along with the "feelings" that make a person want to be intimate, a couple's bond of trust will have been damaged when an affair comes to light. In order to be truly intimate, you must have trust in a relationship. Additionally, it's difficult to feel amorous when there are also probably feelings of betrayal, anger, hurt, and more in the mix.

Affairs may also lead to comparisons, which are odious. The aggrieved partner will have a very hard time not wondering if the "other" lover was better in bed or more attractive. Affairs are a megawatt hit to the self-esteem of the cheated-upon person. Even if the reason for the affair was something else at its core, the victim of infidelity always suffers a loss of self-confidence.

If the affair was an attempt to get the other partner to take notice, that also usually backfires. It's the equivalent of setting up a jealousy test and saying, "See, other people want me so you should too," only to have the aggrieved partner read that as she's not pleasing her partner or that the adulterous partner is no longer into the relationship.

With all of these sexual entanglements surrounding affairs, you might think that no couple would ever recover from a sexual infidelity. However, it is possible. Both partners need to put a lot of work into rebuilding the relationship before they once again reach a truly fulfilling sex life.

An Aired Affair

So what happens when the victim of the affair finally discovers the transgression? Whether it comes to light accidentally or even through an admission of guilt, the result is obviously going to be a period of tumult and reassessment for the primary couple. Do they try to work it out? Split? Point fingers? Share culpability? The questions will be many and the interactions that follow will be heated.

When an affair transpires and is then discovered, the way that it is handled immediately after that may determine the direction the primary relationship goes. Basically, when the offender and the offended end up in confrontation there are two main reactions that will make things worse:

1. **Withdrawal**. In this situation the offender or the offended will pull away and circle the wagons. If you are having too many conversations with yourself, you are probably not having enough with your partner.

2. **Eruption**. In this scenario, there is an emotional eruption. If you are screaming, hurling insults, and looking to vent without concern for the impact it will have on your partner, chances are you're unwittingly damaging the relationship even further with your volatility.

The problem with either of these reactions is that they are extremes. Typically when you are trying to be rational and assess a situation to see if it is reparable, "extreme" is not the way to go. Honesty is fine. Honesty with yelling and screaming is futile.

If a couple does find themselves face to face with sexual betrayal, the following steps will help them get back on track, or at least enhance the probability that they will survive the transgression if that is the direction they choose to go after working through the immediate disappointment and anger implicit in the initial airing of an affair. Follow these steps in order to increase your chances to work things out.

There Must Be an Apology

Before any discussion, an unequivocal apology is in order. No excuses, no "but"s, no mitigating circumstances. The apology should sound something like, "I am incredibly sorry that I behaved in an irresponsible manner. I betrayed your faith in me by deceiving you and I damaged our trust." It should not be something like, "I'm sorry you're upset about my affair, but if you were more open-minded sexually I wouldn't have been tempted to look elsewhere."

The former is the statement of an adult who realizes that he is in charge of his life, and recognizes that his actions have consequences. The latter is the statement of a boy who still believes that he is a victim of other people or circumstances. Unless he flips his perspective and begins to accept some responsibility for his behavior, the chances that he will be a trustworthy partner are near zero.

There Must Be In-Depth Discussions

Following the sincere apology, there must be open dialogue about the situation. The discussion, or more likely a series of discussions, should begin with the goal of understanding the basis for the destruction of trust and the transgressions. Basically, the couple needs to ask, "Why has this happened, and what must happen to prevent a recurrence?" Understanding the root of this relationship breach (and the corresponding damage of the couple's bond and trust) does not guarantee that it won't happen again. However, unless the couple is expecting a miracle, it is unreasonable to assume that an affair is a one-time event and will not recur without addressing the reasons it occurred and formulating a prevention plan together. As we mentioned, affairs are rarely simply about attraction to another person; they are more likely an embodiment of other dysfunctions within the primary relationship as well. Genuinely happy couples don't typically stray.

Once a couple has communicated about an affair, if there is a desire to try to repair the relationship, the work will begin in earnest. Trust will have to be rebuilt bit by bit and the relationship will spend some time on tenuous proving ground until a solid foundation can be reformed. This is also one case where coupling physical trust and reparative work with the emotional can definitely enhance the process.

The Offender Must Admit to the Transgression

A critical action on the offender's part, as reassurance that her efforts to restore trust are sincere, is her willingness to delve into herself, confront the personal issues that led to trust breaches, and acknowledge them openly and responsibly.

Make an Ironclad Agreement to Cut Off Contact with the Lover

It is not uncommon, sometimes despite best intentions, for an affair to continue after discovery. This is especially likely if the lover is someone the affair-involved partner works with or has regular contact with through some other circumstance. Other arrangements (job change? shifting to another department?) have to be made. Otherwise it is like a recovering alcoholic taking a job as a bartender—the temptation is too much. What's more, the aggrieved will likely suffer on a daily basis if her partner is having contact with the person involved in her heartbreak. In other situations where there is not close proximity to the lover, calls, notes, and any form of contact must end—without exception.

Sexual Solution

Rather than be one of those couples that allow an affair to be a cancer that infiltrates and irreparably damages a relationship, create a reconciliation that uses the symptom, sex, to heal the breach. Think of it as physical homeopathy or like healing like.

The Healing Genital Massage

As we've seen, betrayal in the form of an affair is a heartbreaking trauma. According to some behavioral scientists—those that help people return joy to their lives by employing techniques of bodywork—traumas are stored in our body's muscle tissues and build up like armor, cutting off energy. The intention of armoring is to defend the body against vulnerability.

However, subtle body armoring also cuts us off from the experience of pleasure. Some of us have experienced the release of energy when a friend gives us an authentic hug, bringing us to tears or even during a massage when the touch of a stranger releases a surge of blocked energy leaving us emotionally drained.

Our genitals are as prone to armoring as the rest of our body. As a result of an affair discovered, the trauma to both the offender and the aggrieved is likely to be a major storehouse of negative imprints, greatly reducing our potential for sexual pleasure.

In men the armoring can take the form of penile insensitivity or, at the least, a decrease in libido. Armoring can also take the opposite form, an attitude of sexual greed or an excessive need for genital stimulation, which fails to bring sustained fulfillment. For women, tissue insensitivity is also common as is painful intercourse due to vaginal tightness or stiffness and, as with men, loss of libido or compulsive sexuality.

When the genitals of both men and women are healed they become more sensitive, vibrant, and more receptive to lasting pleasure than previously. What's more, it also opens both partners to an attitude that promotes healing of their breach of trust in this most sensitive area of their lives.

The focus of genital healing is a gentle exploratory as well as probing massage of genitals. The goal is to soothe the subtle tensions that have been picked up by the genitals as a result of relationship insults, specifically the hurts that occur as a result of an affair. For whomever is the giver, the mantra throughout the experience is, "I'm here to support you," as the massage proceeds.

In both the female and male experiences, the goal to bear in mind is the healing and release of emotional injury that has entered the genitals. However, the experience may also be arousing to the point of orgasm. It is wise to consider that a by-product of the experience, rather than the goal, since focusing on orgasm may not provide the necessary attention to the healing experience.

It is important that both partners have a readiness for this very powerful and intimate experience. Consequently, this is not an experience for the early days of an affair's discovery when emotions are strong and raw. Rather, this is an experience that will bring peace and soothing to the heart and soul of a couple toward the latter part of the healing process.

HEALING GENITAL MASSAGE — FEMALE VERSION

If the woman is to be the initial receiver, follow this directive for a successful, supported experience.

Step 1

Prepare. In order to provide a comfortable experience for the female, her partner should prepare by washing his hands, cutting his nails, and applying a generous amount of water-based lubricant to his hands. The female partner should position herself by lying on her back, unclothed, of course, with knees up, legs apart, and her head supported by several pillows.

Step 2

Proceed with caution. The male partner is to begin by gently and slowly massaging his partner's inner thighs, gradually moving toward her vaginal lips and then proceeding to lightly stimulate her clitoris. He is to be guided by his partner's response as to how he proceeds with his gentle exploration of her genitals. She may lift her pelvis toward him, twist away from him, or make sounds of pleasure or sounds that suggest he back off.

Step 3

Enter with care. It is important for the giver, the male partner, to respond sensitively to his partner's cues. If she is receptive, and indicates that he can enter her, he can do so with one or two fingers, again, depending on the reception he receives. Once inside he should massage the inside of her vagina slowly and gently, moving from left to right, and then circling the vaginal walls. If the female partner experiences pain or tension, she should ask her partner to remain still within her as she breathes slowly and deeply. When the tension is released, she should instruct her partner to continue his gentle exploration.

Step 4

Breathe, process, feel. If the female partner experiences more tension, she should follow the sequence of stopping and breathing deeply as many times as is necessary. While this is occurring the receiving partner may experience a range of emotions, including sadness, anger, negative flashbacks, all of which need to be accepted by her partner.

Step 5

Go deeper with guidance. When some of this interaction has occurred, and if it has gone well, the giving partner should move his fingers deeper into the vagina. In contrast, while it is normal for the receiving partner, especially the female, to express apprehension at some stage of the massage, if the moment of concern does not pass, she may not be able to go further at present. The experience should be discontinued and picked up at another time.

If the experience continues, the male partner should not only continue to be sensitive to his partner's cues as he continues his vaginal massage, moving deeper and deeper, but he should also ask for guidance as to his movements, when to stay in an area longer, when to move on, when to go faster, slower, softer, or firmer. It is important for the female partner to give voice to her experience as the massage continues.

Step 6

Find closure and comfort. The experience ends when the woman expresses that she is ready for his fingers to be removed. It is best that she doesn't do so under pressure, but as a result of feeling comforted and comfortable that she has been massaged lovingly in this very sensitive part of her body, and that the tension in her vagina has been dissipated. After her partner has removed his fingers, the receiving partner will probably need some time to relax and integrate the healing experience.

HEALING GENITAL MASSAGE— MALE VERSION

Roles may be exchanged right away or postponed for another time. When it is the male partner's turn to be the receiver, follow this version for a connected experience.

Step 1

Prepare. The female partner should prepare in a similar manner as her partner did—wash her hands, shorten her nails, and apply a generous amount of water-based lubricant to her hands. The male partner's position is similar to the position his female partner took, lying undressed on his back with his legs apart, his knees raised, and his head supported by pillows to his level of comfort.

It is important to note that when the male was in the active role as the receiver, he was probably more comfortable and confident. In the receiving role, it is likely that he will feel more vulnerable and perhaps insecure, so the giver should proceed slowly and offer continuous support.

Step 2

Start softly and slowly. The giving partner begins by stroking the front of her partner's body slowly and gently before approaching the genital area. The male's genitals are nestled in an almond-shaped space supported by bony structures in front and back. The genitals are attached to the bony structures by tissue and most particularly by pelvic floor muscles, which will be a major focus of the healing massage.

Step 3

Make genital contact. After stroking the front of her partner's body and doing her best to remove any tension, the female partner should gradually move down to the genital area. Start with the area between the scrotum and the thighs. With one hand gently lifting the scrotum, the other hand is massaging the muscle structure from the edge of the scrotum down to the perineum, the area of sensitive tissue beginning at the scrotum and continuing to the anus.

Continue along that path, gently and slowly, using the lubricant to slide along and remove tension. Gradually move down toward the perineum. When massaging the perineum, while continuing to lift his scrotum, use a firm, but still gentle pressure, going back and forth along the length of the perineum.

Step 4

Spread the wealth. Massaging the perineum and the surrounding area is the main focus. Continue in this area until you get feedback from the receiver that he feels a release of tension. The receiving partner will also appreciate occasional stimulating of his penis since this will create a balance between releasing tension and experiencing sheer pleasure. Lastly, at the base of the penis—between the penis and the scrotum, there is a small muscle mass that can also be massaged for tension release.

Step 5

Bring the massage to a close by lightly caressing and stroking the whole body and kissing deeply. Allow the receiving partner time to bask in the feelings of being nurtured and supported. This type of sexual healing will bring intimacy back into your sex life since it is about caring, trusting and connecting . . . not just the physical action of sex.

Chapter

11

THERE'S TOO MUCH CRITICISM AND BLAME

It's not me, it's you. Sound familiar? Relationships are a tricky road of reciprocal interaction between two people but the successful ones long-term are not the ones that end up with finger-pointing and name-calling in the mix. In fact, relationships characterized by criticism and blame are bound to end in dissolution or unabated distress. And when criticism becomes chronic, especially if tainted with sarcasm or contempt, well, there is no happy ending.

One of the first things to disappear in a troubled relationship is politeness. As laughter and validation disappear, nitpicking and pain tend to surface. When couples communicate in a blame-oriented way, they instantly create a major obstacle to openness and effective relating. Nothing will squash romance faster than the ego blows that result from continual criticism. Unfortunately once this interactive pattern begins between two people, it can be difficult to get communication back on track as partners quickly lose sight of the bond that brought them together and instead find themselves caught up in negative thoughts and feelings.

The thing to remember is that relationships are supposed to be mutually beneficial and supportive. When they slip from secure to strained, however, it should not be surprising that any future issues encountered will become increasingly difficult to surmount. The important thing for a couple to try to avoid is letting their relationship shift such that the only way they know how to effectively relate is through blame, because relying on that as a communication dynamic is a surefire ticket to the demise of their relationship.

Relating, Responsibility, and Acceptance

Okay, remember the old adage "It takes two to tango"? Well, it also takes two to taunt. When chronic criticism and blame come into play in a relationship, chances are the root is not just about something one partner finds annoying that is easily rectified by pointing it out. No, usually it has to do with a myriad of things that manifest as "Well, it's your fault" when really the underlying issue has less to do with culpability and more to do with who is taking responsibility for their own actions.

Frequently the motivating factor behind blame and criticism is an issue that the blamer doesn't want to take responsibility for. The man or woman who points the finger is likely hiding something behind that finger. Often the unspoken dynamic behind the criticism goes something like this: "I'm uncomfortable so I need you to change in order for me to feel better." The issue may be anything from shyness ("Why did you leave my side at the party?") to neatness ("You're such a slob!") but the criticizer avoids their own issue—dealing with his shyness or need for order—by assigning blame to an outside source rather than recognizing his own part in the situation.

Finger-pointing is one very clever way of enacting the denial principle. If the criticizer truly convinces herself that it is "you and not me," then she can more readily protect the sense of self. No one wants to think that there is something wrong with them or that they are the one to blame for a couple's issues.

That said, those who do step up and take responsibility for their own culpability are the ones who are more likely to have rewarding and reciprocal relationships. This is because there is a parallel process in our journey through life. One track is the acceptance of one's love partner. Each of us wants to be loved and accepted for the person we truly are. We do not relish the energy of criticism and blame directed toward changing or "fixing" us; we hunger for the freedom to be our authentic selves. Criticism and blame does not address or feed that hunger. In contrast, those elements are more likely to result in the hiding of our true selves from the criticizer, which will definitely put a damper on a relationship, emotionally and intimately.

The other track of the journey involves embracing ourselves—accepting our strengths and weaknesses—without exception. This is where personal responsibility comes into play. Some may think that accepting yourself will lead to sloth and avarice as well as other deadly sins, but the opposite is true. Those people who have eliminated self-criticizing inner conversations from their heads are more at peace and more likely to behave in accord with their positive view of themselves. In contrast, those individuals who fill their minds with self-hate have a propensity to behave in accord with those thoughts. They tend to be angrier and less compassionate, not only toward themselves, but towards others as well.

By taking responsibility for your own actions and accepting not only one's love partner "as is" but also oneself, there will definitely be a minimization in the amount of criticism and blame cast within the relationship. This is especially true if *both* partners in a relationship learn to take responsibility for their own actions (if only one partner does so, you may still have a disconnect as the "responsible" partner may suddenly find himself getting the short end of the stick too often). That said, on the whole, the more that acceptance is promoted within your relationship, the less blame will be assigned.

Misplaced Fault-Finding

Though taking responsibility and mutual/self-acceptance can go a long way towards healing a critical rift in a relationship, there are a few other scenarios that should be discussed because they may require slightly different tactics when negotiating the who's-to-blame terrain.

Family Issues

To begin with, sometimes criticism and blame are the products of ghosts from days past. By this we mean family-of-origin issues. People come into an adult love relationship with sensitivities from their family. If the model with which an individual has been raised is one in which criticism and blame factored highly into the family dynamic, then some of these mannerisms may be intrinsic to the individual due to examples viewed while growing up. For instance, a critical father could be the model for a young child, and then in turn, that grownup child takes that model into her adult love relationship. Therefore, the individual may be highly critical of her partner but not recognize it as destructive behavior because it's what she was socialized to understand as "normal." It also may have the opposite effect and make her particularly vulnerable to criticism.

In this situation it's also important to assess the aforementioned responsibility factor. While upbringing does not let someone completely off the hook for their adult behavior, it can be an important piece when deciphering how you relate as a couple. Accepting how your past may affect your behavior in your present is also part of responsibility. If criticism and blame are ruining your adult relationships but you recognize that this is a dynamic you learned from bygone days, the act of understanding (or desiring to understand) where this impulse comes from can help you to do the work necessary in order to make changes in your relations with your love partner and move your dynamic in a more conciliatory direction.

Misplaced Anger

There is also the possibility of displaced anger manifesting as blame and criticism. Sometimes criticism and blame at home result from unresolved frustrations outside the primary relationship that surface where they shouldn't, since the individual facing the crisis has not effectively found another venue in which to work out his issues. For example, let's say a person has a hard time at work and instead of dealing with it assertively at the office, she comes home and works out the distress on a mate. This is a self-sabotaging situation because the very person that is supposed to be there offering support to the angered partner who comes home needing an outlet, is the one who is now being belittled and blamed (and will likely feel little incentive to support his mate when she needs it since he's just been attacked). Misplaced emotions are very dangerous because outside forces can ruin otherwise perfectly healthy relationships if not dealt with in the proper venue (where the issue is actually taking place, not at home). It is important to keep these extenuating circumstances in mind when working to minimize the amount of criticism and blame between you and your partner. Knowing from whence the fault-finding between you stems will help you zero in on the real issues at hand and move more quickly towards resolution without assigning blame. What's more, having the courage to share your self-understanding about where some of the blame and criticism is coming from will strengthen the connection with your partner. Doing this is a bold and honest counter to hiding behind the pointing finger.

Sex and Criticism/Blame

There is no room for finger-pointing when it comes to sex. A truly mutually satisfying sex life requires an environment that encourages giving, exchange, and positivity in order to flourish. Mix that with the insecurity that comes from too much criticism and possibly even the sadness and confusion that results from too much blame and the result can be a sexual shutdown. Who would want to be truly intimate and connected with someone with whom they were at odds or who made them question their own self-worth?

It is hard enough to allow oneself to be emotionally naked with a partner, but throw in physical nakedness and it ratchets up the vulnerability another notch. If partners don't create a supportive environment for this state of undress (which may be the result of things going on outside their sex life), then it will be that much more difficult for them to communicate positively between the sheets.

Closely tied to the issue of blame is its opposite, acceptance. When two individuals enter into a sexual relationship, what they are really seeking (besides carnal satisfaction) is that feeling of being close to someone—knowing someone is there to have them, hold them, and take them as is. If that is missing, it is very difficult to feel satisfied sexually. You can get it on until the cows come home and still be left empty.

This brings us to another factor that is closely related to acceptance but is often underappreciated: emotional safety. In a love partnership where lovers get extremely intimate with each other, feeling emotionally safe is essential, especially if the couple desires the sexual relationship to be open and full rather than inhibited and cautious. Blame and criticism hurt. To think that the wounds from those kinds of assaults will somehow disappear when crossing the threshold into the bedroom is, at best, naive. Couples have a responsibility to each other to create a "safety net" around their relationship. If they fail to do so, creating instead a "Gotcha!" atmosphere, they will miss out on the full spectrum of benefits they could enjoy from each other, both in and out of the bedroom.

There is also a Catch-22 element implicit in the criticism/ blame/sex triad. If the criticism and blame in a relationship end up directly tied to your sex life, then you will definitely notice a disconnect in your between-the-sheets behavior. For example, if you begin blaming your partner for a less-than-scintillating sex life, then she will likely start to feel insecure and wind up inhibited. In other words, criticism will do nothing to bring you two closer and it definitely kills libido. The divide will just increase as your inability to create an intimate environment is hampered by your critical intimations.

Blame in the bedroom will effectively lead to a nonsupportive atmosphere where acceptance of individuality is questioned rather than explored and enjoyed. A better bet is to try to build a sexual safety zone in your relationship so that you and your partner can feel at ease with each other when in your most vulnerable intimate state.

Stop the Insanity

Nothing is going to be solved between you and your partner if both of you are constantly screaming at each other or silently sulking about who is to blame. Pointing out each other's weaknesses instead of championing your individual and mutual strengths really defeats the entire purpose of being a couple. Shouldn't it be about celebrating the things that drew you together more than spending your time tearing each other down?

The trick is to learn to snap out of it. When faced with a finger-pointing scenario, resolution is unlikely unless one partner is willing to take on-the-spot initiative. Sure, you can wait and address the issue later—after you've likely stewed on it for a while and it's taken on a life of its own, becoming an even bigger issue than it ever should have been! Or, you can take the bull by the horns and start making changes in your behavior and how you relate as a couple in the moment.

Typically in the blame-counterblame trap, both partners issue their complaints about unwanted behavior—usually in the form of a verbal onslaught—but do nothing to address the issue. They fail to take action so the same scene is played out in reruns and continues to demoralize them both. For example, consider the situation where one partner—let's say the female partner for this example—is always running late. In the typical blame-counterblame scenario, the male partner paces, fumes, blames, and criticizes while he waits for the female to get ready. "Why are you taking so damn long?" he laments. She will defend herself against his onslaught with complaints of her own: "Stop pressuring me, I don't do that to you!" Neither takes any action. Of course, since this is an activity in reruns, she could start her readying earlier. He, however, could take matters into his own hands, leave at the appointed time, and meet her when she arrives rather than continuing to rant at this tired little drama. To do so might seem harsh, but it is far better than hurting the relationship by issuing mutual rants about an issue that does not warrant so much energy, and negative energy at that.

This is just an example and may not be the tack you wish to take, but the idea is that if you let things fester—arguing endlessly about them without taking any corrective action—there is no chance of breaking the cycle of mutual recrimination and restoring the opportunity for productive relating in the future.

Along with this just-don't-stand-there-do-something concept, here are some other ideas for how you can improve the level of acceptance within your relationship while putting the lid on criticism and blame (or at least tipping the balance in favor of positivity).

Practice the *I* Word

To avoid covering up your own issues with the pointing finger, consider beginning your statements with a form of the pronoun *I* (*me*, *my*, *mine*). *I* statements are expressions of responsibility; beginning a sentence with *I* personalizes your feelings or thoughts. Note that tacking a prefix like "I think that you . . . " or "I feel that you . . . " onto a sentence does not make it an *I* statement. An *I* statement is a report of your awareness of yourself, not the other person: "I prefer orderliness and would like your help with that," rather than "You're such a slob!"

Ditch Your Negative Thoughts about Each Other

One of the most fruitful tasks a couple can take on is to do their best to stop negative mental thoughts about each other. Even if those mental musings are not made overtly, the thoughts themselves discourage relational passion. Rather than "awfulizing" the situation and/or telling yourself, "How could he (or she) feel this way?" accept the present reality. Quiet yourself instead of exacerbating your emotional state and losing perspective.

One of the best ways to do this is to get behind your partner's behavior and try to understand it, rather than condemning it. Feeling understood promotes connection, being criticized leads to alienation.

Squash Your Self-Loathing

Next time you realize you're putting yourself down, take a moment and think about what you're doing. Then try to reframe the situation, turning it into positive self-talk. For example, instead of "Man, I look so fat in these jeans today," flip the focus onto something you do like such as "Wow, I'm having a really good hair day." Just a simple shift in thinking will make it more difficult for you to criticize others as well. Remember, acceptance of yourself and your partner is one of the most effective steps towards minimizing the effects of criticism and blame within your relationship.

Weave a Safety Net

In order to make a safe zone in your relationship, make sure that when you are in an intimate/romantic situation, you point out to your partner that you are grateful they are there with you and willing to be so close. By setting up an acceptance scenario, the receiving partner will feel more warmth towards their partner rather than competitiveness or even worry that they're not "pleasing." This is important in emotional areas of the relationship, but also when getting intimate.

Remember You're a Work in Progress

To foster acceptance and diminish criticism and blame in your relationship it is often helpful to remind yourself that you (and your partner) are a work in progress, ever evolving, always learning, and fallible. Perfection is not for humans. In fact, some couples have tried a little experiment that has proved quite powerful in their journey to be more self-accepting and compassionate with each other. The experiment involves writing a letter of forgiveness to yourself. Each partner is to look back at a regrettable action they have committed, recall who they were at the time, and write a letter that expresses disappointment with the behavior, but forgiveness and understanding toward themselves. After composing the letter, both partners read their letters aloud to each other and discuss it. Typically, this type of experience fosters both self-acceptance and the acceptance of each other as fallible, but maturing individuals. What's more, by considering behavior regretful, but not considering the person regretful, an important distinction is reinforced. While behavior can certainly be disappointing and negative, human beings are too complex to be labeled as negative based on one behavior, unless it is heinous, which is rarely the case.

The bottom line is that each of us has the capacity to change. When we assign responsibility for our malaise to another person, we impede our change potential and render ourselves powerless. Taking responsibility for whatever complaints you have is the way to go, and playing that out on the sexual stage will reinforce your gains.

Sexual Solution

Criticism and blame do not belong in the bedroom. Acceptance and love do. In order to promote an intimate atmosphere where both partners in a relationship can feel secure (i.e., remember the concept of promoting a safety zone within your relationship), it is important to be able to share your most intimate sexual selves with each other without fear of judgment. With that in mind, the following sexual solution will help foster a supportive pleasure principle within your pairing.

WATCH YOUR PARTNER SELF-PLEASURE

For most people the practice of self-pleasuring is a private experience, done alone. The practice of self-pleasuring in the company of your lover is something altogether different; it is a delicate challenge. Exposing your most intimate erotic behavior to your partner is likely to trigger feelings of insecurity and vulnerability. The challenge for the partner who is watching is to be accepting and supportive while this very intimate activity is being shared.

This experience is designed to counter lack of acceptance and excess criticism that might take place in a relationship. As each partner exposes herself and each is given the opportunity to be supportive and accepting under these very intimate conditions, an atmosphere of love and mutual closeness is created. The biggest victory here is when a loving attitude is carried into the relationship, making it feel safer and more accepting.

Self-pleasuring in front of your partner has additional benefits. You are learning to stay with your feelings of pleasure in the face of a partner that, in the past, has been critical. Doing so strengthens your ability to believe in yourself, to realize that your report card of yourself is the ultimate judgment.

What's more, self-pleasuring in front of your partner will also provide you with the opportunity to break the taboo of self-pleasuring secrecy. You are making the statement, "I am a sexual being, and I have nothing to be ashamed of"—a statement that can carry forward as confidence in your relationship. Last, the experience is also an opportunity to learn what is pleasurable to your partner. How your partner stimulates himself, the touch, pace, rhythm, strokes are all there for you to observe.

Take the following steps for a mutually satisfying self-pleasure share session.

Step 1

Cover your eyes or not. The experience can be done initially with the self-pleasuring partner wearing a blindfold, to cut down on self-consciousness, and then at another time without the blindfold. Or, the experience can be completed without a blindfold, right at the beginning. Each partner is to make his or her own choice, and needn't make the same choice of how to begin. The important thing is to decide what will remove inhibitions the most effectively in this situation.

Step 2

Pick a partner to go first. The partner who is self-pleasuring is fully unclothed and in a position that is comfortable. It can be standing, lying down, or in any position that is desired.

Step 3

Don't go straight for the sex-pot. Both partners, when they have their turn, do not have to move to the genitals directly. They should touch their bodies in the way they like to be touched. It's important to show what "foreplay" you engage in before masturbation as well since it is all part of the self-pleasuring process. Ideally, the partner who is self-pleasuring will be free to make whatever sounds and breathing patterns that are natural.

It is also best if he or she self-pleasures as they ordinarily would, and does so in an unhurried manner, focusing on his or her own sensations as much as possible, rather than being distracted by self-consciousness.

Step 4

Ditch self-denigrating thoughts. Remember, this is about acceptance. So, if the self-pleasuring person starts to feel his or her thoughts leaning towards, "What is she (or he) going to think of me?" the focus should be shifted to the idea that it is his or her self-acceptance and pleasure in this scenario that is important, not anyone else's.

Step 5

Offer encouragement and support. The partner who is observing should mainly focus on the self-pleasuring partner's courage, and offer acceptance and support—an acceptance and support that will hopefully be committed to memory and later brought out of the bedroom and into the external relationship to counter any excess criticism and blame. As a delightful aside, the observing partner is also privy to intimate details about his or her partner and will be learning how to sexually please the self-pleasuring partner, which will enhance future coupled sexual activities.

Step 6

Embrace the experience and your lover. When the self-pleasuring partner is finished, give your partner a few moments to gather his or her emotions. Then, the self-pleasuring partner should lie close with the observing partner. Next, the observing partner should take his or her lover into their arms, offering words of support and appreciation. Then switch roles. When both partners have shared the experience, stay unclothed and discuss what took place. Keep the focus of the discussion positive and supportive. Make a pledge to interact more positively, not only in the bedroom, but throughout your relationship.

Chapter

THERE'S NOT
ENOUGH AFFECTION

See me, feel me, hear me, taste me, touch me. When it comes to really knowing someone, it's important to want to know all of them. And in order to do so, one must engage the senses. It is about liking their scent, admiring their look, kissing to taste, and appreciating their touch. All of these sensory perceptions are included in the concept of coupled affection—showing adoration towards one's partner. But all too often, people forget the importance of demonstrating their feelings of fondness in a tangible way. And even though their love may be solid, if there aren't manifestations of affection in the mix, chances are a couple may start to question their connection.

Affection has many degrees (mild, medium, *hot*) and couples usually find their way to a temperature and style of affectionate interaction that suits them as a pair. It may also vary from situation to situation (e.g., a couple might be less affectionate in public but all over each other once they get behind closed doors). The important thing, however, is that both partners get what they need as far as feeling the security that comes from knowing one's significant other is truly concerned with their well-being. That is usually evidenced through demonstrations of affection, both physical and emotional. It is about remembering that your partner is probably not a mind reader and therefore some responsibility falls to you (and vice versa) to make sure that your lover knows the depth of your feelings. How that is shown and to what degree it surfaces is malleable, but if there is no affection in a relationship, then one of the primary reasons for being together as a couple is lost.

Intimate relationships are meant to provide a source of closeness and adoration that is unattainable in other places in one's life. You may have friends galore, colleagues, an active work/social life, and so on, but a partnership offers a different element that those other relationships and interests do not. The affection of a romantic partner brings something different to the table, but it must be apparent in order to truly be appreciated. Hidden affection may be there, but if a couple doesn't know how to effectively express their adoration for each other, their connection may suffer. With that in mind, it makes sense to explore how affection may best be expressed, and what male/female expectations of such entail.

Affection in Action

"You know I love you, right?" Guess what? She might not. While the surface answer given by the recipient of such a statement might be "Yes, of course," chances are just the utterance of that as a question might indicate there is not enough affection being shown in a relationship. Or, it might allude to the fact that there is not enough security that the relationship is solid. While we wish to believe that things in our romantic life are on a good footing, the only way we truly get a sense of this is if our partner is affectionate. This can mean through verbal affirmations or physical mannerisms, but the bottom line is if affection is not somehow displayed, confusion may result.

Humans need affection. One of the ways this manifests clearly is through the sense of touch. Touch is a powerful affection-enhancing action. There is a need for body contact within all of us; think caressing, fondling, cuddling, embracing, and stroking. Although touch itself is not necessarily affection, touching and being touched often leads to affectionate feelings.

Couples forget that tactile stimulation is a crucial relationship resource. Not only do humans have an innate hunger for physical affection, but it's also a powerful communicative device. Sometimes words may not express what the simple brushing of a hair from a partner's face will convey. Or think about the instant sense of security that is felt when holding hands with fingers interlaced. In adults, the need to be held, touched, and cuddled, like other needs, varies in intensity from person to person and in the same person, from time to time, but it is present in all of us—and is especially crucial in our romantic relationships. Touch fulfills an intrinsic need for attachment that all humans crave and one of the best places to get this need met as an adult is from one's romantic partner. Relationships that involve affectionate touching tend to thrive; those devoid of physical contact wilt.

Despite the desirability, and perhaps because of the potency of touching, it is unfortunately often neglected in adult interactions. Part of this may have to do with our socialization outside of romantic relationships. When you consider the role computers, cell phones, Blackberries, and other forms of impersonal contact play in our daily lives, it's not surprising to note that sometimes an adult can go an entire day without having any physical contact with another human being. Add that to the sexual harassment concerns that surface in many office situations, and it's not hard to see why so many of us have become "programmed" to avoid touching or to confine it to a few permissible circumstances such as sex, athletics, casual greetings, and aggressive expressions.

This is highlighted by the results of an experiment conducted some years ago by Professor Kenneth Gergen and his colleagues in the Department of Psychology at Swarthmore College. These researchers found that when persons were introduced into a pitch-black room in which there were half a dozen strangers, persons they knew they would never meet again, more than 90 percent touched each other on purpose and nearly 50 percent hugged each other. In contrast, almost none of the participants in a similar group made any sort of tactile contact in a lighted room.

The experimenters were struck by the desire of their dark room subjects to make contact; given anonymity, a group of perfect strangers moved very rapidly (in about thirty minutes) to a stage of intimacy seldom attained in years of casual socializing. It was concluded from these findings that people share strong yearnings to be close to each other, but that our social norms discourage us from expressing these feelings physically. The tape playing in our head may sound something like: Don't touch him; he may get the wrong idea.

Unfortunately, this societal barrier to touching may permeate other areas of our lives—including our romantic encounters—making it more difficult for adults to touch each other comfortably outside of overt sexual scenarios. However, if there is a lack of touch in a day-to-day relationship for a couple, it definitely makes it harder for them to transition to sexual intimacy. Their bedroom behaviors will likely be mired in inhibitions carried over from their outside interactions.

Also tied in with this is the fact that it is not permissible for many men to touch each other freely so they may be more careful about their physical affection, or how often they show it. Essentially, guys are socially encouraged to touch only during sports and sex. What they've learned the rest of the time is likely not to touch each other. Therefore, those little signs of physical affection that mean so much to a woman may not come naturally to a man. He may be fighting years of being told to "act tough" every time he reaches out to graze his partner's arm. That constant struggle can lead to a physical disconnect for a couple and they may not even be sure why.

This may also translate into public displays of affection (PDA). Sometimes couples find themselves at odds on this issue—one partner is fine with it and the other feels uneasy. This may also go back to the social norm issue. For example, if a man is uncomfortable with showing his affection physically in public because that is what he's been led to feel is appropriate but then is all over his partner in private, it may confuse her or lead to a disconnect. She may feel like "Well, obviously he has feelings for me because he can't keep his hands off me at home, but is he ashamed of me since he won't kiss me in public?" This kind of issue will definitely lead to discord between two partners and is something they must discuss. If they don't, the miscommunication will continue to fester and the less-touchy partner may not even realize that his behavior is bothering his significant other. What this illustrates, however, is that sometimes showing affection also signals to the receiving partner that they are the "chosen" one above all other possible individuals and when that message is not conveyed clearly through gentle displays of physical contact, then it may cause consternation. The affection needs to be visible to the receiving partner, of course, but sometimes they also need the world to see it too.

Tell Me/Show Me You Love Me

Women need to hear it. And when men are affectionate they tend to show it, behaviorally. It's an affection disconnect. Many couples find themselves in a state of coupled confusion where they both think they're demonstrating their affection effectively, but they're not—thanks to differences in the expectations and mannerisms of the sexes.

For example, women tend to be very verbal. They want to talk about their feelings, they'll openly discuss their emotions and therefore they tend to assign credence to words. But when he doesn't say the words she needs to hear, she may start to worry that things are awry in their relationship.

He, on the other hand, is likely action-oriented and may think he's given her very clear signals about his affection just by the things he does. In other words, "I washed her car every Saturday this past month and took her to dinner afterwards. What does she mean she doesn't know I care?" Men tend to demonstrate through behavior, except ironically not always through "touch" as we previously discussed. However, they do frequently attempt to show their feelings through "touching" hey-that-was-really-sweet behavior. That is, through indirect, thoughtful behavior that, for them, conveys affection and caring.

This subtle difference in how the sexes tend to speak/show affection has led to more than one couple's meltdown. For this reason, it would behoove men and women to try to recognize the subtle affection symbols that their partners offer up on a regular basis because it is in the recognition of those clues that the true depth of their feelings lie.

One thing to keep in mind is that emotional affection (as opposed to physical manifestations like touch), may be expressed in a variety of ways. It is not just saying "I adore you" or "You mean the world to me" (which are nice things to hear by the way), but it is also in remembering to give compliments to each other. *Sincere* compliments that is. People can tell when they're being handed empty words versus those that have meaning behind them. Don't say it if you don't mean it, but if you do mean it, don't forget to say it!

Thoughtfulness also comes into play here. Do you remember the little things? One sure sign of affection is looking out for your partner's well-being and making sure that his needs are met. This goes a long way towards demonstrating feelings that run deep. If you didn't care, why would you bother to make sure your partner was comfortable? People respond to feeling cared for.

This is also closely tied with respect. Couples who are respectful of each other want their partners to thrive. Remembering to show your partner that you honor and respect them as an individual by demonstrating politesse is another means of showing fond attachment (though one should not be too polite since that may actually stifle affectionate behavior). Supportive statements such as "Hey you're doing a great job!" or "Wow, you're amazing and I so appreciate you being here" are also very powerful when it comes to making one's partner feel needed (which in turn also fosters feelings of fondness towards the compliment giver).

Then there is the magnetism of flirting. Little sassy moves or flirtatious maneuvers are a constant reminder between partners that there are strong feelings. Teasing falls in this same category. Think of the first grade boy who pulls his crush's pigtails. He does it not to hurt her but rather to get her attention because he likes her. As long as these kinds of overtures are kept in the playful category, they're healthy and fun demonstrations of shared devotion.

Basically, all of these examples show how affection may play out in a relationship. You can get a sense just by reading them if your relationship is rich with overt expressions of affection or if perhaps you and your partner are withholding your feelings and demonstrations thereof from each other. If men can become more aware that sometimes women need verbal affirmation of their fondness (i.e., Just *say* it!) and women can learn to occasionally show their love as well (i.e., Just *do* it!), there may be a better communication between the sexes about just how deeply their feelings run.

Sex and Affection

At face value, it would likely seem that sex and affection go hand in hand. However, just because two people get physical doesn't mean that they necessarily know how to show affection towards each other. And if demonstrations of emotional and physical affection are not present outside of the bedroom, transitioning to a connected sexual experience is going to be difficult at best.

Essentially, the desire for feeling affection with one's partner during sex goes back to the need for love trust and love within the relationship. Never is this more important than while being intimate because of the natural vulnerability that comes with this kind of closeness. Therefore, if there is affection in the mix before you hit the sheets, it is easier to let any walls come tumbling down when the clothes come off.

If outside the bedroom demonstrations of affection are in full swing, correspondingly a couple's sex life is more likely to be full as well. However, if affection in both forms—emotional and physical—is lacking, sex is going to be superficial and perfunctory. It's kind of like what is happening in the kitchen (not literally just the kitchen, but you get the point), is going to reflect in the bedroom.

Interestingly, a lack of affection outside the bedroom may also encourage an individual to agree to sex just because they are hoping to attain the affection they crave through the act of making love. This illustrates the frequently held adult misconception that simply the act of having sex shows affection. Unfortunately, that is not always the case. People can have sexual relations and still be left feeling very empty. But, that doesn't stop adults from trying to find comfort through copulation.

In an interesting study done by Dr. Marc H. Hollender and coworkers at the Vanderbilt School of Medicine, researchers showed that for some women the need to be held or cuddled is a major determinant of sexual behavior. In-depth interviews revealed that many women engage in sex with men when their real desire is simply to be held. As Hollender and his colleagues stated in the journal *Medical Aspects of Human Sexuality,* "The desire to be cuddled and held is acceptable to most people as long as it is regarded as a component of adult sexuality. This wish to be cuddled and held in a maternal manner is felt to be too childish; to avoid embarrassment or shame, women convert it into the longing to be held by a man as part of an adult activity, sexual intercourse."

The point here is that people oftentimes confuse a need for affection and touch with a need for sex.

As for men, many of whom we already discussed are hesitant to touch other men except when engaging in athletics for fear of being seen as demonstrating "unmanly" behavior, their hesitations are often similarly disguised when relating to women. That said, it would not be risky to surmise that men as well as women long to be held and caressed without having to be sexually involved. It is apparent to most observers, though, that men have an even more difficult time than women acknowledging and satiating their hunger for touch. Because of this, sex becomes the major means of satisfying that urge (i.e., it's the only way they know how to reach out and touch within acceptable adult boundaries). Unfortunately this also leads to the familiar lament of many women, "He touches me only when he wants sex."

A woman may feel, for instance, that her guy barely pays attention all day and then all of a sudden (and it may be sudden), he's ready to make love. It cannot be that abrupt (straight from no affection to intimacy) and end up a truly connected, giving sexual experience. The point here is that foreplay (we actually prefer the term *loveplay*) starts when you open your eyes in the morning, not just when you are aroused.

Upping the Affection Quotient

If your relationship is affection-challenged the first step towards increasing your affection-quotient is obviously recognition. If you and your partner are unaware of the diminishment of your devotion demonstrations, there is no way that you'll effectively work towards rectifying that lapse in your relationship. It's okay to even bring up the situation with little comments such as "I sure miss the way we used to walk along holding hands all the time when we first met" or "I know how much we love each other, but if once in a while you could surprise me with those three little words when I'm not expecting it, it would mean the world to me."

It's about figuring out what *you* need in order to specifically feel the affection you crave from your partner. Everyone responds to different affection cues so it would make sense for you to spend some time figuring out what really makes you feel loved, safe, warm, cared for, and so on. Then, focus on those gestures when you are given the opportunity to voice what you need.

Once you've done that, consider the following as a means of strengthening the signs of overt affection—emotional and physical—in your relationship:

Set Up an Affection Account

When trying to balance the affection you give versus the affection you receive in your relationship, think about a relationship account. Similar to a bank account, there are deposits and (inevitable) withdrawals. The deposits are forms of affection. The withdrawals may be the little irritants that occur with couples such as one partner forgot something, was ten minutes late getting home, got silly drunk, and so on. If there is a surplus of deposits that buffers the withdrawals, that could close the account.

If at some point you realize that you are constantly irritated by every little thing your partner does (or vice versa, your partner is easily irritated by you), it may be an indication that your account is overdrawn and you both need to work to replenish your "sentiment savings." In other words, instead of being constantly furious with each other (or at the very least detached from lack of affectionate exchanges), consider how you both might increase the emotional and physical affection in your relationship. With a little work, you will likely find that the balance ends up back in the positive.

Practice Nonsexual Touching

Each day, touch your partner in a nonsexual but intimate manner. This may include a warm hug, an arm around the waist, a shoulder massage, caressing your partner's hand, playing with your partner's hair, and so on. A perfunctory peck on the cheek will not do; it is not a substitute for a warm embrace, nor is a conventional handshake capable of replacing a caressing hand. The idea is to offer loving, giving, affectionate forms of touch to your partner and hopefully vice versa. By removing the taboo from affectionate yet nonsexual forms of tactile expression, you're likely to find yourselves opening up more and more to the idea of shared affection (with each other and the world around you as well). Try to keep track of when and how you touch and the way you feel yourself respond to received touches during your day. And don't be afraid to share with each other what you like, what makes you feel supported, and what stimulates your affection-quotient towards your partner.

As you work to incorporate more overt emotional and physical affection into the construct of your relationship, you will also benefit from reconnecting on a sensual level in the bedroom as well. The heightened state of intimacy will allow you to make quicker gains in the affection department if the groundwork is laid properly and the sentiment between you and your partner is real and supportive. Get ready to reawaken your senses and enhance your affectionate connection.

Sexual Solution

It is apparent that couples who minimize affectionate interaction—exclusive of sexuality—are at risk of "losing touch" with each other. Besides the pleasures and satisfactions that come from the feel of a loved one's skin, touching provides an emotional link between intimates.

It may well be that after ignoring our desire for affectionate connection, we are left with a vague sense of dissatisfaction but are not able to place a finger on its source.

Affection starvation, as with prolonged hunger for food, may eventually wane as a couple gets used to an unaffectionate state of existence. But this does not mean that the need is gone, only that the "pump must be primed" in order to (literally) return them to their senses.

THE SENSUAL EXPERIENCE

Recall a special day in your life. It may have been a celebration of a holiday, an occasion such as your birthday, or any day for whatever reason, you were showered with love. Remember the warmth, sense of security, and solidarity you experienced as you were blanketed in affection. This is the kind of experience the activity of sensual touch is going to evoke. It is going to be a celebration of touch that will remind you of the value of affection in your relationship, and it just may take a surprise turn.

Step 1

Set the scene. The partner who is going to take the lead in this experience, the giver, should arrange the space where this is going to take place so that it is sensual. Make sure the air is warm; consider using a special incense to bring a fragrance into the air. Arrange soft lighting, perhaps with candles, and play some music that is supportive of this sensual experience.

Step 2

Get ready to touch. The goal of this exercise is to take turns caressing each partner's entire body (try this at least once a week). Take a shower together, go to bed without clothes, and have the receiving partner wear a blindfold and lie on his or her stomach. The blindfold is used to make it easier to focus on the touch sensation without distraction.

Step 3

Stroke the skin. With utmost gentleness, as if never having touched before, the giving partner is to begin with the back of the head, ears, and neck, caressing gently and tenderly, then moving down the back and sides, down the buttocks, inside the thighs, legs, and feet. This experience is not a massage. The connection is exploratory, not the kind of physical, kneading stroke of massage. The giving partner should visualize his or her hands radiating warmth and love. Feel free to make little circles on the skin's surface alternated with long, deep strokes. This can generate an energy leaving the receiving partner's skin feeling effervescent. A light, warm body oil may be used if desired.

Step 4

Be open to feeling. The receiver is to concentrate on his or her feelings. This is very important. It is important that the receiver not get caught up in worry that the partner is tiring as he or she touches. The receiver should be reminded to stay with his or her feelings, and give feedback during the experience only if something feels particularly pleasant or unpleasant. Otherwise, discuss the experience *after* it is over. At that time the receiving partner can instruct the giving partner as to touch preferences (lighter, harder, slower, faster) for future contacts.

Step 5

Flip over. After a while (usually twenty minutes or so), when the back of the body has been completed the receiver is to turn over and the front of the body is caressed in the same way. Start with the head, face, and neck, slowly and gently and with sensitivity—as if blind and "seeing" with the fingers, moving to the chest, belly, and sides. Massage the thighs, legs, feet. As with the back, caress the front until either partner has had enough.

Step 6

Switch it up. After one partner has been sensually touched, it's important to change places such that the giver becomes the receiver. This allows both partners to experience giving and receiving tactile affection and promotes balance in the relationship as well. This is especially important if a couple finds themselves in a situation where one person typically does more giving than the other.

197

Step 7

Play Slip-n-Slide. When both partners have taken turns at each of the roles—giver and receiver—take some body oil and lightly massage your partner all over. When you are sufficiently slicked up, stand close to each other and explore every possible way of slipping and sliding around each other with the undulating movements of two lithe cats cozying up to each other.

Next, one partner should lie down while the other slides over him or her, slipping and sliding over as many body parts as sensually and seductively as possible. Using hands, feet, face, arms, legs, even genitals, gently rub over as much of each other's body as possible while keeping the experience simultaneously playful and erotic.

Step 8

Finish it off. For many couples, their newly resensitized bodies may have built up a charge of sexual energy that begs to be released. If so, maintain the tactile stimulation and come together toward completion. For all participants of this experience, the value of tactile affection has been introduced into your memory bank. Periodically repeating it will likely result in an atmosphere where daily gestures of affection come naturally.

Chapter

13

WE EXPECT EACH OTHER TO "MIND READ" OUR NEEDS

Wouldn't it be nice if your partner just knew what you needed all the time? If at precisely the right moment he would just be there with the perfect compliment or item or whatever without you even asking? Dream on. Even the most communicative of couples are unable to completely anticipate each other's needs.

The desire to have one's needs met, however, is deeply rooted in your past. The concept of mind reading may well be a vestige of childhood. At that time in your life, you expected your parents to anticipate your every need, perhaps before you were even cognizant of what you wanted. As adults, however, we must be responsible for our own needs. That's part of what it means to be a grownup. But in that same vein, if our needs involve our partner, it is up to us to speak up. Unfortunately, we all-too-often don't.

The problem is that within silence lives a major precipitating factor for relationship failure. While it may be commonplace in this day-and-age to gripe about "communication problems," many couples—influenced by the images of romantic love promulgated in our media-driven culture—believe that they should be inextricably linked to their partner through an innate understanding and sensitivity. In effect, they say, "You ought to know how I feel or what I mean if you really love me." Realistically, however, this is often not the case.

You Should Just Know Me

Do you and your partner *really* know each other? Chances are you will answer "yes" right away if asked this question. Chances are a better answer would be "sometimes." Human beings are mutable. People change, ideas change, thought-processes change—that's how we grow. So to say that you unequivocally know your partner is to put a bit of a damper on the possibilities for growth within your relationship. And to expect your partner to know you and anticipate your every need also puts that growth-barrier on you. The only way your partner could possibly meet your every need would be if you never changed your mind about anything. Pretty limiting, right?

Yet, some would contend that being in a relationship allows them the privilege of being less forthcoming in their efforts to communicate than they might be with casual contacts precisely because their partner knows them better (and therefore presumably can fill-in-the-blanks when things are not communicated perfectly). The only problem with that theory is that if you're using your communication skills more effectively with strangers than you are with your nearest and dearest, well, soon your partner won't be your closest confidant any longer.

Additionally, people in relationships tend to consistently overestimate the ability of their partners to anticipate their behavior (and vice versa). Research has supported the claim that closeness does not automatically equal comprehension. Even in the simplest predictions of one another's behavior, couples are usually wrong.

In a report published in *Marriage and Family Living*, researchers asked spouses which one of them would tend to talk more during a decision-making process dealing with how they would spend a hypothetical gift of several hundred dollars. The session was taped so that the actual amount of talking done by each could be measured. Only seventeen out of fifty individuals correctly predicted who would be the more active speaker. What's more, after the session was over and the participants were once again asked who talked more, over half still judged incorrectly.

In another study, investigators increased the participants' motivation to predict correctly by showcasing a myriad of "prizes"—gloves, scarves, lingerie items, belts, and wallets. If, without communication, they could successfully coordinate their choices—that is, choose the same item—they would receive the items as rewards. They all failed. Not one of the twenty-five participating couples succeeded in predicting one another's choices on as many as five of all twenty items.

In still another study, this time involving 116 couples, each partner was asked separately to give the names of persons considered by both partners to be close mutual friends, not including relatives. In an astonishing result, only six couples were in total accord on this task. One couple even failed outright, completely disagreeing on their mutual friends.

What this illustrates is that while couples may claim to know each other like the back of their hands, chances are they're pretty frequently off the mark. That said, and studies aside, it should not be surprising that couples who engage in solid communicative efforts are happier and more sexual than those who make no concerted efforts to understand each other. In fact, a major feature in relationships suffering from a lack of intimacy is not a discernible lack of attraction between the partners but more likely a deficiency in their communication skills. In discordant relationships, there is usually a marked failure of both partners to express and be attuned to each other's feelings and thoughts.

There may be any number of reasons a person might have an inability to "speak up" including coming from an uncommunicative family (which might mean inadequate development of verbal skills), shyness, lack of self-confidence, intimidation, controlled hostility (in which an individual may not communicate in an attempt not to "blow up"), suspicion, self-protection, and so on. Whatever the reason, most often the deterioration of communication occurs gradually and is the result of an interactive process. For example, sometimes a partner will encourage communication and then discourage it by frequent interruptions, in effect, disqualifying the speaker and her message. Or perhaps one partner will ask for more communication only to then feel like the other partner is "nagging," which consequently leads to harbored resentment. The bottom line is that there is only one route to a truly happy relationship and that is through communication, not ESP.

Sex and Mind-Reading Needs

There is no doubt that talking about sex is tough. If it were a piece of cake every couple would have an amazing sex life. But on that same note, expecting your partner to just figure it out or automatically know what works for you is also totally unreasonable.

Still, when it comes to sex, most people tend to live by the credo "No news is good news." In other words, if neither partner says anything, they tend to assume that their partner is okay with what is going on. Unfortunately, that is frequently miles from the truth. Sex is a highly intimate and vulnerable exchange. As a result many people are terrified to speak up about their needs for fear of hurting their partner's feelings or possibly even worse, turning their partner off.

Women tend to have a particularly difficult time asking for what they need in bed because some women still believe they are supposed to focus on their partner's pleasure rather than their own, and oftentimes their goals during sex are less about climax and more about closeness. So she just hopes and prays that by being sexually conjoined to her partner she will somehow get the intimacy she craves and that he will somehow figure out what would make her feel good without direction. Thing is, the phrase "different strokes for different folks" applies here; no woman or man comes with a roadmap. So what might have worked with one partner in the past won't necessarily be pleasurable for a new partner. Unless there is a dialogue about the situation at some point, neither partner will know what is truly working and what is not.

Reading physical cues may give some couples information (i.e., if they seem to be sexually turned on then they assume things are good). One thing to keep in mind, however, is that there are a lot of good actors out there as well. People will frequently fake sexual pleasure in order to enhance their partner's self-esteem or perhaps enjoyment of the experience. But this kind of behavior is usually to the detriment of one partner's pleasure as well (the "acting" partner).

The basic point is, you're an adult. Adults are responsible for their own needs. Likely, your partner is not going to be able to read your mind, so at some point, you're going to have to get over it and talk to each other straight up about your sex life. By not doing so, you risk remaining unfulfilled. If you don't create a roadmap, you're likely to get lost.

Speak and Spell It Out

So what's the opposite of mind reading? Spelling it out! The more you learn to actually articulate your needs to one another, the clearer your communication as a couple will be (and the less chance there is of either one of you harboring unspoken frustrations).

Practice Asking Politely

Your partner may not know what you need because you aren't in the habit of verbalizing it. Work on incorporating direct, clear requests into your relationship when you can. For example, if you're too cold from the air conditioning, instead of just saying "Wow, it's cold" and then hoping your partner will turn down the AC and getting mad when they don't, try finishing off your thought with a request. For example: "Wow, it's cold. Would you mind turning down the AC, or if you're comfortable in this temperature, could you get me a blanket I can curl up under?" That way you have requested what you need in clear terms instead of expecting your partner to anticipate them.

Test Your Beliefs

Rather than relying on your untested assumptions, find out if what you think about your partner is true. In other words, instead of thinking you might be a mind reader and assuming you know what your partner is thinking, ask! Make it a habit to begin sentences with "I assume" when trying to assess your partner's needs. For example, "I assume you hate visiting my parents" or "I assume you are happy with our social life outside our relationship." You can also turn this into a way to help your partner learn what is important to you (e.g., "I assume you know how critically important a promotion is to me"). By seeing if your assumptions are accepted or refuted, you can learn a lot about each other (assuming that there is honesty within your answers).

Institute a Better-Late-Than-Never Policy

All of us are inclined toward afterthoughts. We often give a lot of thought to our delayed reactions to an experience, but we don't necessarily share these important delayed responses. In actuality, these "percolated" responses may be very important and it will benefit us and our relationships to give them voice. This is also important because sometimes we might be feeling okay about an experience but upon reflection realize it was something we didn't wish to do again. However, if your partner only has the first part of the information, he will not know you've changed your mind on the subject or activity and that can lead to major misunderstandings when going for a repeat scenario (this is especially true in sexual interactions).

Once you've begun to institute more open discussion of your needs and how they might be met with your partner (and vice versa—how you might meet her needs), you will be ready to carry that conversation into the bedroom, a notoriously tenuous talking ground.

Sexual Solution

Expecting your partner to know what you want without having to make a request—while reasonable on some occasions, such as passing you the towel when you come out of the shower, for example—is by and large unreasonable as a rule of existence. Nowhere is shyness about speaking up more common, and sometimes more troublesome, than in sexuality. To counter a pattern of expecting your partner to meet your needs, we suggest a dialogue that will allow you to speak about your sexuality in a playful, but powerful manner. The experience will allow you to give voice to your hidden sexual desires, as well as to any part of your sexual experience that you would like changed. Combining two sensitive areas, sexuality and honesty, will be a challenge. Once you have been expressive in this area, however, you are more likely to bring confidence to other, less challenging aspects of your life.

THE SEXUAL GRAB BAG

The following experience will allow you and your partner to talk to each other about your sexual interactions and needs through a self-created game. To create your playing pieces, take ten sheets of paper, folding them into eighths, and cut along the folds so that you have eighty paper playing pieces on which you can write brief notes. Have each partner grab about half of the playing pieces and go to separate parts of the room to write.

On each note, both partners should scribble down as broad an array of sexual preferences as they can each brainstorm separately. Some examples may include preferences like: *I love when you go down on me; Rough sex really turns me on; My favorite is when we're making love with rear entry; Talking dirty when making love is hot;* and so on. Include only positive preferences and include whatever you can think of even if the preference is not one you personally favor. Notice that the preferences are gender neutral. The pronoun "I" or "me" is stated but whether it is one partner or the other stating the preference is purposely left open. You don't have to use all eighty playing pieces but this gives you lots of room to play, or pieces to pitch in the trash if you decide you don't like an idea.

Now come together and put all the preferences together in a bowl. Game on.

Step 1

Get naked and comfy. Begin by having both partners undress and sit opposite each other, either on the bed or against a bunch of pillows. You want to be comfortable since it will allow you to share more openly. Sit opposite each other.

Step 2

Take turns picking a note from the bowl. The partner who first reaches into the bowl and chooses a note randomly should read the note aloud and comment as to how well this preference is in sync with his or her sexual preference. The speaking partner is encouraged to elaborate and the listening partner is welcome to ask for clarification if needed. There is no time limit on any discussion that ensues and after the speaking partner is finished, the listening partner is welcome to engage in a dialogue about his or her thoughts on the issue. Alternate which partner pulls from the bowl and begins the discussion every time.

Step 3

Provide a sex summary. After going through the variety of notes, each partner is to summarize his or her understanding of their partner's preferences. There should not be judgment within the context of this but merely a repetition of what each listening partner thinks he or she heard their partner's preferences to be. This is an important step so that there is not miscommunication in what is actually being favored.

Step 4

Get touchy-feely with each other. After the discussion, both partners are to caress, stroke, and thank each other for the dialogue in any manner they wish, including of course, experimenting with each other's sexual preferences, as long as both partners are receptive.

Chapter

14

WE AVOID ISSUES

See no evil, hear no evil, speak no evil. Many couples attempt to cruise through their relationships with this well-known phrase as their "Really, everything is absolutely fine" mantra. Unfortunately just ignoring issues will not make them go away. If anything, issue avoidance makes sure that things are absolutely *not* fine.

It is in the sweep-it-under-the-rug syndrome that many couples find themselves involved in a faux relationship of sorts. On the surface they pretend that everything is dandy, keeping up a terrific ruse for all those with whom they come in contact. Unfortunately, this performance, which is also frequently an attempt at fooling themselves, will eventually fall flat. Every relationship harbors issues, every couple comes upon impasses, and every twosome is imperfect. Unfortunately, those who avoid their issues entirely by pretending that everything is peachy in order to keep the peace at any cost are setting up a scenario where ultimately their pacifist environment will also be void of verity.

Simply put, consistent perfect harmony within a relationship is unrealistic and highly unlikely. Just the very event of sharing space and time together limits an individual's personal choices. Add this to the fact that both parties in a relationship will undoubtedly have some differing interests and preferences, and you can see how relationships provide fertile ground in which the seeds of conflict can flourish. This does not mean that brawling as a means of issue resolution is advocated, however. Instead it is just meant to illustrate that issues within a relationship—whether deep-seated or superficial—are inevitable and must be recognized. To completely avoid or deny the undercurrent in a relationship is a definite way to deaden it.

Confrontation Circumvention

No one likes confrontation. Well, perhaps we should qualify that—there may be a few people who thrive on it professionally or in competitive scenarios. But no one likes confrontation in their romantic life. That is the one area that is "supposed" to remain happy, loving, supportive, and conflict-free—or at least that's the fantasy version. The real-life landscape is usually at least a little more contentious.

Still, many couples think they should be able to achieve and maintain a relationship rich with warmth and closeness without the sometimes exhausting and downright frustrating friction that comes from continuous interaction with another human being. Unfortunately this unrealistic expectation leads to relationship breakdowns. If both halves of a couple don't recognize that sometimes relationships are work, you may have someone bolting out the door saying, "Well, ultimately it wasn't right," when in actuality the relationship may have been a good fit. It was the fantasy of a relational utopia that was skewed.

On the other side of the coin are the individuals who stay with a relationship that has issues, but are so confrontation-avoidant that they keep quiet rather than face off with their partner. In this case, however, issue avoidance leads to unvoiced grudges that are kept hidden from their partner because the desire for smooth sailing outweighs their wish for issue resolution.

Unlike individuals who are excessively and indiscriminately critical, confrontation-avoiders are unwilling or unable to express their displeasure toward their partner. They are reluctant either to place definite limits on what they will and will not tolerate or to resolve the issues between them for fear of rocking the boat. And the fear runs so deep that sometimes they even try to convince themselves that whatever is bothering them isn't really an issue. You'll catch the terminally confrontation-avoidant saying things to themselves like, "Oh, it really doesn't matter anyway," or going so far as to dismiss the fact that a problem even exists. In other words, denial is a very powerful tool, but not a very helpful one.

In most confrontation-phobic individuals, the person chooses to withdraw rather than confront the problem and risk an uncomfortable situation. This may be the result of a lack of assertiveness on the part of the withdrawing partner, or perhaps a fear of losing their partner. The individual then keeps quiet at the expense of her own happiness. She might also use issue avoidance as a protective barrier that keeps her from getting too close and risking further intimacy with her partner (which she might unwittingly equate with potential emotional hurt).

Whatever the root, the confrontation-avoider refrains from telling his partner of his displeasure with the way things are going between them. While the avoidant partner may think this is creating an environment for peace, the reality is that the partner is actually more likely setting the relationship up for a blowout instead of dealing with smaller issues head-on when they arise.

Also, where there is smoke there is usually fire. In other words, don't think for a second that the other partner is perfectly, blissfully happy with the way things are going. Typically if one partner is feeling dissension, the other feels it too. Their issues may be divergent, but it is not often that the displeased partner is alone in her unhappiness; the other partner is often aware of the unhappiness and has his own dissatisfaction as well. But if the other partner is staying similarly quiet about their issues as a couple, then he is complicit in the coverup.

The result is that the relationship becomes a conspiracy of silence. Neither partner is speaking up, or perhaps one is speaking up and the other is staying quiet with the more dominant partner allowing (and perhaps secretly desiring) the quieter one to keep silent. The rub is that optimal relating requires checking in to make sure the relationship is satisfactory to both.

Another danger of issue-avoidance is that it can be a catalyst for couples to grow apart. Although they appear to share common goals, their "arrangement" is based on a false vision. In this case the "shush conspiracy" they have fallen into allows each to veer silently off in a different direction instead of allowing them to grow together as a unit. Their issues become a wall that starts to gain height with each issue they quietly agree to ignore. Indeed, the failure to deal constructively and compassionately with differences and the issues between a couple is the single most powerful force in relationship deterioration.

Sex and Issue Avoidance

Without a doubt, a couple's sex life will not be without issues. Perhaps one partner likes it rough, the other more connected. Perhaps one partner enjoys toys, the other prefers erotic movies. Or maybe one partner's sexual history is practically chaste while the other's is borderline promiscuous. The result is that any two people falling into bed in essence agree to have a hypothetical sexual negotiation as soon as their clothes start coming off. If either partner stays mum for fear of offending or losing their partner, then the couple has issues.

The goal of a sexual relationship should be mutual pleasure and when couples lose sight of that goal for whatever reason, their sex life will suffer. And if two people find themselves in a relationship that has issues outside of the bedroom that are not being voiced, those issues will follow them into the bedroom and you can sure as heck bet that any issues they've got sexually are not being discussed either!

Sexual interaction puts two people in an already heightened state so when issues do cross the threshold into the bedroom but then remain unspoken, feelings get hurt. Because of the intimately vulnerable situation that inherently comes along with sex, issues that arise in this area are often closely tied to personal preferences and complexities, which may make it more difficult for partners to try to discuss any discordance.

Openness, self-revelation, and putting feelings forward in a straightforward manner can be the force that prevents the buildup of an insurmountable sexual fortress. In other words, every sexual issue—minor as well as major, long-term as well as brief—involves some emotional reaction. Whether the emotion evolves into alienation or increased sexual connection is predicated on how it is approached.

For some couples, unresolved issues—sexual and otherwise—lead to what could be termed an emotional divorce from each other. This unfortunately may mean that the issues will promote an attachment disconnect from one's partner (making it virtually impossible for a connected sex life). The convenience of the relationship may be preserved, but the feelings of closeness once there will fade. This may lead to partners seeking temporary relief outside the relationship by engaging in an affair (which could be viewed as a desperate search for an emotional connection somewhere since the tie in the primary relationship is suffering). It could also lead to a couple reinforcing this faux relationship they've established by trying to derive satisfaction from outside activities—overzealous socializing, for example—to mask the lack of sexual connection they have within their relationship. The longer that a couple remains emotionally divorced from each other, the more their sex life will suffer as well. It's a vicious cycle because couples that do not deal with their issues on a routine basis will likely find themselves pulling away from each other, sexually and otherwise.

Whatever the manifestation, the result is that an issue-avoidant couple is not likely to be a sexually fulfilled couple.

Bring It Up!

While issue avoidance results in relationship dissatisfaction, this is not to say that uncensored self-expression is synonymous with relationship bliss. Indeed, there is a wealth of information to suggest that unedited communication may be more than any relationship can bear. Remember, feelings can be easily hurt within the context of a relationship owing to the heightened sensitivity and vulnerability that stems from opening oneself up to another person emotionally and sexually.

If there is indeed a connection between self-expression and relationship satisfaction, it is not linear in nature. Too much or too little disclosure may be associated with discord, while some intermediate amount, under appropriate conditions, is related to happiness. Before an issue is brought up for discussion, it is vital to consider factors like timing, interest and receptivity of the other person, validity, appropriateness, and the effects of the disclosures on either partner. Once those things are assessed, the first step towards breaking out of an issue-avoidant pattern is to make sure that issues are brought to the forefront of your relationship *before* they become insurmountable. As with any communication challenge, however, there are ways of getting there that will be more productive than just blurting something out without any forethought. Keep the following thoughts in mind the next time you recognize that an issue within your own relationship might need addressing.

Choose Getting Better over Feeling Better

Thinking about approaching your partner on a sensitive issue is, in a way, like other sources of anxiety—it is easier and more comfortable to avoid. However, in many ways that is limiting—we are instructing ourselves to remain stuck in our comfort zone. Feeling better is a short-term approach, but pushing past the initial anxiety is a long-term strategy that pays off through a stronger relationship and a more satisfying sex life. What's more, in time, emotional muscle develops and approaching potentially touchy issues gets easier.

Open with Empathy

Rather than avoid sensitive issues, begin by considering your partner's view of these issues and giving voice to them when you speak to her. Think about your partner's side of the equation; consider what her reaction might be to your words and how her response might vary predicated on how you phrase your requests surrounding the issue. If your partner feels understood it is much more likely that she will be amenable to hearing your view on a sensitive issue, and less likely that it will result in a nasty confrontation.

Schedule a Weekly Love Relationship Meeting

Make it a habit to "check in" with each other on a routine basis. By doing this you will have a forum for discussing issues, and both you and your partner will be emotionally prepared for any touchy issues that are between the two of you that need to be discussed. That is, rather than "springing" an issue on each other at a bad time, knowing that the meeting is set, there is an emotional preparedness that happens almost automatically in anticipation. You can make the habit even better by scheduling some loving/shared time after your weekly meetings so that you don't leave the meeting with negative feelings (e.g., perhaps plan a delicious dinner out each week after your forum, but let the discussion be finished before you move on to the corresponding positive phase of your meeting).

Discuss the Avoidance Issue with Your Partner

Rather than avoid sensitive discussions and then avoid the avoidance—bring it up. Ask each other in advance, "How would you like me to approach sensitive issues? When is the best time? What is off-limits?" and so on. By laying the groundwork before you have an issue to voice, you are paving the way for a more receptive partner (and a better mutual exchange) when you do have to face something. Plus, by giving you "instructions" your partner is no longer the "silent" partner in any issue you need to bring up. You can always use his words to start the conversations (e.g., "Remember when you said if I had something I needed to discuss with you, this situation would be the best scenario? Well. . . .").

Choose Your Medium

If the prospect of a face-to-face confrontation is frightening for you, perhaps a handwritten note, e-mail, or some other medium will make it easier for you to bring up the issue. Perfect is not necessary; doing it is! Rather than avoiding something because it makes you nervous, find a means of at least opening the discussion that is less anxiety-producing for you. The goal is to get the issue on the table. How you accomplish that is up to you.

Say What You Mean, Don't Say It Mean

The discussion of sensitive issues will pay off in a stronger relationship and a more exciting sex life, but the discussions will not go well if they are used to vent resentment. When bringing up an issue, be empathetic as noted above, but also refrain from intense finger-pointing. The best way to approach issues is to focus on the pronoun *I* and its variants, rather than the blaming pronoun *you*. Talk about how an issue is impacting you, rather than how dastardly your partner has behaved. Quite simply, "blunt and brutal" honesty seldom facilitates intimacy. Real intimacy is experienced only when each member of a couple has the capacity and wisdom to be sensitive to his or her partner's feelings.

Once you have begun to get more comfortable with eradicating issue-avoidance from your relational repertoire, you will then be better able to extend the discussion to include your sex life. Sex is perhaps one of the top areas of issue-avoidance for any couple, but also one of the areas that will benefit most from openness and honesty between partners.

Sexual Solution

Closely tied with issue avoidance is fear. Fear of confrontation, fear of judgment, fear of loss, and probably most influential in the romantic arena, fear of rejection. But if two individuals in a sexual relationship let fear paralyze their coupled communication, then their intimate time together will eventually become nothing more than an elaborate coverup of all the issues permeating their relationship outside the bedroom. With that in mind, there's no better way to zap issue avoidance in the sexual arena than to lay those fears out on the table (or the bed as the case may be in this situation).

DISCUSSION OF SEXUAL FEARS

This experience is designed to not only get the dialogue between partners started about issues in the sexual arena, but also to promote trust and respect while doing so (both of which are integral to a fulfilling sex life as well, since you can't have a mutually reciprocal sexual relationship without some honesty and openness in the mix). Get ready for some sexual sharing.

Step 1

Ponder your sex secrets. Think of one sexual fear that you are receptive to (although perhaps apprehensive about) to discussing with your partner. For men, it may be about responding issues, like climaxing too quickly or erection concerns, or perhaps not feeling confident in satisfying your partner. For women, common concerns are that your body is not attractive, that you take too long to climax, or maybe that your partner won't stimulate you the way you want.

Step 2

Pick sides. Partners should sit facing each other with strong eye contact and decide who is going to go first. If need be, toss a coin. Then, the first speaker is to be asked by his or her partner, "What are you afraid of in sex?"

Step 3

Share something sexual. The responding partner should describe one sexual fear he or she has clearly and directly. Then the responding partner should take a few minutes to give some background and history of the fear, how it plays out and impacts the relationship, and how it impacts him or her emotionally. The speaker may take as much time as needed.

Step 4

Listen well. Throughout the sharing of the fear, the listening partner is not to interrupt and should resist the temptation to be defensive. The listening partner's role is to understand, not to explain. The listening partner may see things from a different perspective, but his or her job is not to convince the sharing partner of his or her view, but rather to be supportive of the speaking partner's courage in sharing a sensitive issue, rather than avoiding it.

Step 5

Respond and ask again. After replying in a supportive, understanding manner, the listening partner is to ask, "Are there other sexual fears or concerns that you want to speak about?" The speaking partner may then speak of another fear, if there is one. Once again, the listening partner will not interrupt, but will listen and respond with support and understanding.

Step 6

Switch speaker/listener roles. Once the speaking partner has expressed his or her fears, the listening partner now takes a turn speaking of sexual fears. The former speaking partner, now the listener, follows the same response style as was applied when he or she spoke.

Step 7

See a sexual resolution. After both partners have had a chance to give voice to their fears, both should close their eyes and visualize how their sexual coupling unfolds with these issues resolved, or at least diminished. See the lovemaking occurring vividly with a positive perspective. Everything is flowing beautifully, lustfully, and lovingly. The tension of underlying anxiety is gone. Reinforce the positive imagery.

Step 8

Practice image/body sharing. When the "short film" each partner has created is playing without interruption by negative images, both partners should share how their "film" is evolving. When both partners' images of a healthy, supportive sexual relationship are in sync (i.e., they're both able to see their sexual fears dissipated and their positive view prevailing), they should share a lovemaking experience that celebrates their courage to face rather than avoid a sensitive issue.

Chapter

15

WE'RE TOO CAUGHT UP
IN OURSELVES

Me, me, me. We're definitely caught up in a world that supports the concept of "self-importance." Unfortunately, when individuals get mired in the land of "me," they may forget about the overriding construct of coupledom—"we."

When entering into a relationship of any kind you have two individuals coming together for some purpose. In a romantic relationship that purpose should revolve around love, support, and genuine caring for one another. At least, that should be the goal. A romantic relationship is not usually entered into with a desire to hurt each other, or a wish to exist in a vacuum devoid of connection and attachment to one's significant other.

Still, other agendas often get in the mix and muddle the relational reciprocity. If one partner or the other is in the relationship primarily for the satisfaction of their own needs (sexual or otherwise), chances are this is not a true partnership. The best relationships find a healthy balance of give-and-take between the participating individuals, but when too much self-involvement creeps in, it starts to look a little more like take-and-take as each partner fights for their "fair share." And once this kind of dynamic begins, instead of a supportive situation, the relationship may start to resemble a competition. In other words, the one who manages to take the most from the relationship wins. In reality, when this happens, resentment accrues and both partners lose.

Real Versus Fake Caring

Do you give for your lover or for yourself? It's an important question to ask when in a romantic relationship because within the answer lies the true meaning of caring. Real caring will manifest in a balanced relationship. Faux caring will get you nowhere fast as a couple because it is largely based in narcissism (i.e., you give to make yourself feel good or you do things knowing that they'll ultimately benefit you, not really because they are for your partner).

To better clarify this idea, consider this: Giving and taking are opposites by definition. Giving only in an effort to heighten your "take" defeats the true purpose of giving in the first place. There should be an element of altruism or care involved in an authentic giving gesture. In the other situation, when giving is done to increase the payback, then the giving is really all about the giver and not at all about the recipient. See the difference?

Real or "active" caring means that something is done to benefit another individual without expectation of reciprocity. It's done purely to make life better, easier, or more comfortable for someone else. Or it's done because there is a genuine desire to bring this other individual happiness. And frequently what happens is that it will still come back to the giver, in spades, precisely because it is authentically felt and received, which in turn makes the recipient feel more amorous and giving towards their partner as well.

Fake caring, on the other hand, is goal-oriented. It's giving a gift because it's protocol or because it makes a person look good (which in turn boosts the giver's self-esteem—and it's all back to the "me, me, me" again). A perfect example is the person who buys something they would like for their significant other's birthday. Hello, it's *their* birthday! Wouldn't it be more appropriate to take the other person's likes and dislikes into account? This kind of "caring" behavior is more likely a form of one-upmanship, selfishness, and lack of consideration—behavior all humans are capable of at times. The point is that considering this behavior loving is an expression of self-deception.

Active caring also means there has to be more than hypothetical caring. A clear example of this is the man who says "I would throw myself in front of a bus for her" when talking about his girlfriend or wife, but then consistently cannot remember to help her take out the trash. The grand gesture may sound good, but it's not "active" caring. It's hypothetical. It's just words. If he can't remember to help with the trash, she's probably going to start questioning what would *really* happen when the bus is hurtling towards them.

While active caring is a definite relationship booster, some couples also run into problems when they attempt to demonstrate their concern for each other but in a manner that is off-the-mark. For example, a man gives his partner a new spatula as an unexpected gift, thinking it's practical since they need one. The woman is responsive but inside very sad because all she really wishes for is a bouquet of tulips because they're her favorite flower. It's a total disconnect. The man thinks he's showing his affection by taking care of a practical need; the woman is craving anything but practical.

When two people require different signs that they're being cared for than the ones they are getting from their partner, the inevitable result is that sooner rather than later both partners will start to feel increasingly neglected. The danger in this is that both partners may think they are giving their significant other clear signals of their affection, but the messages have transmission errors. In other words, one partner does not recognize this as a sign of caring and mistakes it for a lack of attentiveness on the part of the other partner. The good news with this scenario, however, is that it's easier to correct than to try and teach someone who is doling out fake caring to substitute that for the real thing. When it's a communication error about what each partner needs in order to feel supported and loved, then opening up dialogue on this issue may help. With fake caring, well, the issues run much deeper.

The bottom line is that active caring does not make a Hallmark movie of the week. Real caring gestures are the everyday things—not grandstanding. It may be changing a light bulb that's out rather than walking past it. It may mean not having to ask your partner for a small favor twice. Active caring is empathy driven and done with the well-being of one's partner in the forefront of one's mind. Unfortunately, many romantic partners get caught up in expectation and in the "What can you do for me?" mentality instead of thinking "What can I do to make your life better?" However, when both partners start to think less about themselves as individuals and more of themselves as part of a collective "we," taking care of oneself becomes synonymous with taking care of one's partner, since they are in essence an extension of self.

Sex and Self-Absorption

A healthy relationship requires active concern on the part of each individual for the satisfaction and growth of the other. And nowhere is this more important in a romantic relationship than in the bedroom! If acts of "loving self-deception" are to be avoided, caring expressions must be developed in consideration of your partner's preferences.

The problems are many when self-absorption crosses the threshold into a couple's sex life, however. It could be something akin to forgetting that there is another person in this sexual equation while in the personal quest for sexual gratification. In other words, "As long as I get off, who cares what else is going on?" is not the mantra for a healthy sex life.

You've heard it before, but it takes two to tango. And of course this applies to the horizontal mambo too. Whatever mating dance you decide to engage in, however, if your goal is a fulfilled long-term relationship with a happy, reciprocal sex life, you must, and we repeat *must*, pay attention to your partner's needs as well as your own.

When individuals gets caught up in their own fantasies or sexual drives at the expense of their partners, feelings are bound to get hurt. Also, it is quite likely that one partner may end up feeling used. And this isn't solved by just making sure that both partners climax. The goal of sex in a coupled relationship should also be heightened closeness. Simply striving for physical release at the expense of connection will not get you there. It turns sex into a goal-oriented competition . . . not an expression of caring.

This becomes glaringly evident when one partner also starts to "demand" sexual acts or exploration. It may be phrased as a "Well, if you really loved me you'd try this" kind of demand, but the bottom line is that it's not really caring behavior. It is manipulation and it makes the other partner feel insecure instead of supported in their already vulnerable state of nakedness.

Basically, an individual can be completely self-centered and make their sex life revolve only around having their needs met, but this type of behavior will lead to an unconnected, unromantic sex life. When caring becomes part of the sexual interaction between two people, however, the give-and-take in their relationship will be heightened, sexually and otherwise.

It's the Little Things

There are many examples of behavior that appears to be caring but is really selfish, or "pseudobenevolent," but rather than dwelling on the negative, we'd like to focus on the positive here. Since the goal in your relationship should be to foster more active caring, it would pay to take a closer look at what active caring means to you and your partner within the context of your relationship and how you might enhance that connection. In that vein, think about some of the following when trying to promote real caring between you and your partner (i.e., less gimme, more giving).

Determine What Your Partner Sees as Caring Behavior

If you'll recall, many couples run into trouble simply because they don't recognize the "signs of caring" that are coming from their partner (i.e., they express caring differently). Rectify this by having each partner ask the other: "What would you like me to do as a means of giving you support and showing my concern for you?" Make any requests specific and positive. For example, remember the spatula/tulip example? In this situation, the woman might say, "I understand when you bring me kitchen utensils it's with the intention of showing you care, but I actually would prefer small, sweet gestures like flowers on occasions when you wish to surprise me. We can shop for kitchen utensils and other practical things together, but knowing you still think of me as 'your girl' by giving me a romantic item like flowers will make me feel cared for." The idea is to verbalize exactly what makes you feel supported and vice versa so you can both work on making those expressions a priority in your relationship.

Institute a Policy of Daily, Active Caring

Relationships take work, but remembering to show affection for one another should be the easy part. Unfortunately in our busy world, many couples forget to demonstrate real caring regularly. Change this by figuring out what little expressions of active caring you both can offer up on a daily basis. These don't have to be done in the same order or even every day (you may alternate between them), but the idea is to develop a repertoire of real, caring behaviors that you both respond to and then use them!

Think remembering to kiss goodnight, picking up a new tooth-brush before your partner needs one, writing a note and slipping it into his work or gym bag for your partner to find during the day. You get the idea. It truly is the little things that count. In fact, many relationships prosper or falter on just that, the little things. Yes, the Hollywood version emphasizes the drama—the affair, for example—but the road leading up to the drama is marred by an absence of small everyday gestures of active caring.

Make Your Relationship a Priority

If you and your partner have been too self-involved lately (or even if you haven't but wish to make sure you stay connected), it's time to reprioritize your relationship. There are many ways you can do this, but consider some of the following:

⚥ **Protect relationship time**. Don't volunteer for extra activities that are mostly ego-driven because it steals relationship time. This is true if you're already overextended to begin with thanks to work or other obligations.

⚥ **Make relationship-promoting decisions**. If work and love are on a collision course, do your best to work out a compromise, but if unable to find a happy medium, choose love.

⚥ **Be resourceful in the name of love**. Don't try to do everything by yourself; get help when you can. Rather than giving the best part of yourself to cleaning and straightening the house, and being drained for your partner, either do the work together or "outsource" some tasks to provide more relationship time.

It is a mistake to assume that individual concerns should win out over relationships. Self-absorption will hinder growth because we cannot expand without involvement outside ourselves. Through relationships, humans learn to look with the eyes of another person, to listen with another's ears, and to feel with another's heart. To simply talk the talk, but not walk the talk will not work. Giving must be sincere and be real rather than superficial. And this includes what happens in the bedroom.

Sexual Solution

Along with receiving sexually, it is important to learn to give. And this doesn't necessarily mean, "I come, you come." What this means is being aware that your partner is a part of the sexual process with you. Sex is about give and take, take and give. By remembering that both of you are involved in the pleasurable process that is intimacy, sex becomes a more shared experience rather than a quest for self-gratification.

One of the best ways to accomplish this is by facing each other during sex (this keeps you from "checking out" and instead forces you to stay connected to your partner). Also, breath play is an extremely powerful way to heighten sensation and the give-and-take atmosphere of a mutually beneficial sexual encounter. With that in mind, we created the following sexual solution to enhance the sharing not only of your sexual selves, but also a key element of life itself—your breath.

SHARING THE BREATH OF LIFE

There is nothing that is as powerful in the realm of giving to each other as sharing the breath of life. The impact is made even more powerful if done under erotic conditions.

Step 1

Brush, floss, and strip. For this experience both partners are naked and the male is sitting in a chair with the female on his lap. This is done when both partners are well—neither partner has a cold or any other illness—neither partner has had a heavy meal, and good dental hygiene has been practiced (halitosis is a serious turnoff here).

Step 2

Practice tandem/tangential breathing. With both partners looking directly into each other's eyes, the experience begins by synchronizing the breath so that both partners are inhaling and exhaling in the same rhythm. Once relaxed into synchronized breathing, the breath pattern should be inverted so that one partner is inhaling and the other is simultaneously exhaling. As with the synchronized breathing, the inverted breathing is very relaxed and relaxing, deep and slow, deep and slow. The rhythm should be harmonized so that it is fairly precise—one partner is inhaling, while the other is exhaling. Direct eye contact should be maintained throughout.

Step 3

Kiss and play. When the inverted breathing pattern is established, it's time to make the experience more erotic by moving closer and teasing with the lips. With mouth slightly open, lips firm but not rigid, the partners should begin to kiss in a light, playful way. After touching lips softly, they should pull away and take turns lightly licking or sucking each other's lips. This tongue play should be alternated with gentle kissing. Each partner's mouth should extend an invitation before the other partner enters. The inverted breathing pattern should still be maintained even as the teasing heightens!

Step 4

Explore more. When one partner is ready for a deeper kiss, his or her mouth will fall open. There should be no forced tongue action. The kissing pace should vary, moving from slow to urgent, hard (but not too hard) to soft. The tongue should be used lightly to explore each partner's mouth. Each partner should feel free to run their tongue over the other partner's lips, or perhaps trace around the inside of their lover's lips and tongue with their own tongue.

Step 5

Go for rescue breaths. With lips touching loosely and the breathing pattern still inverted and in rhythm, both partners should now begin mouth-to-mouth breathing. Because the lips are touching loosely, a little outside air is incorporated into the exchange of air that the partners are providing for each other. There should be a perceptible warm current from the breath that emanates from each partner and they continue exchanging breaths.

For some it takes time to get used to this practice and you may feel as if you are suffocating. If that occurs—to avoid feeling suffocated—simply slow the process and move apart slightly so that extra air may come in through the side of your mouth. In time you will adjust to the process and you may slowly move closer again.

Step 6

Exchange air and energy. Once the mouth-to-mouth breathing is in effect, both partners should try to imagine that they are not only exchanging breaths, but also providing energy for each other. With each exhale, the giving partner is mixing his or her energy with his or her breath and giving that energy-air combo to his or her partner. With each inhale, the receiving partner accepts the gift, receiving his or her energy and combining it with his or her own. It's a reciprocal process of giving deeply and receiving graciously.

Step 7

Rock, aspirate, and penetrate. Along with the breathing the male may begin rocking and rubbing his genitals with his partner's to increase arousal. The female partner may be inspired to fall into the pattern and rock along with her partner. When the female partner is ready, she may reach down and bring her partner inside of her. Intercourse occurs gently and slowly as the inverted and shared breathing continues to climax.

AFTERWORD

You may have noticed, this book isn't like other books on sex. It doesn't present sex outside the context of a relationship and the focus hasn't been simply to arouse. Rather we have encouraged you to explore dimensions of sexuality that many couples miss completely: the emotional part of getting naked together—in a very focused manner. It is our hope that the experience will not only strengthen your sexual intimacy, but your overall relationship intimacy as well.

If we had to summarize our goal briefly it would be something like: It doesn't matter what you have below the belt if there's nothing in your heart to connect it to.

In other words, any sex act can be obnoxious, boring, or downright regretful unless it occurs with someone who turns you on. And in a committed relationship, nothing will dampen a sexual conncection faster than the burden of ineffective problem solving. Heavy and demoralizing are the weight of unresolved differences.

We've addressed this dilemma in a unique manner. Just as combining mind/body elements to solve health issues is the way to go, we have combined relationship issues with sexuality to provide a more powerful remedy than pinpointing either one individually.

We've presented a concept—a new approach that, as far as we know, is original. It features customized sexual experiences to clarify, integrate, and assist in resolving relationship issues that occur outside the bedroom. Our suggestions are just that. Use them, or create your own. We realize that when it comes to sex, different strokes for different folks applies.

Lastly, and you probably get this, so consider it a reminder: Learning about sex and intimacy and keeping both in sync is a lifelong task. Even with years of experience all of us still make mistakes on occasion. Don't give up. The journey is more than worth the stumbles.

ABOUT THE AUTHORS

Photo courtesy of Fred Block.

Dr. Joel Block is a senior psychologist at North Shore–Long Island Jewish Health System where he supervised doctoral interns at the Sexuality Center for over twenty years. He is an Assistant Professor of Psychiatry on the clinical faculty of Einstein College of Medicine and a Diplomate in couple therapy of the American Board of Professional Psychology.

Dr. Block has written for numerous professional and popular magazines including *New Woman*, *Family Circle*, *Working Woman*, *Parents*, and *Newsday* and is frequently sought for print interviews. He was honored in 2003 at Hofstra University as Outstanding Couple Therapist of the Year and is the author of nearly twenty books on love and sex.

He has been a frequent guest on local television and has also appeared on several national television shows, including twice on each of the morning news shows (CBS, NBC, ABC). Dr. Block has also been a featured solo guest on *The Phil Donahue Show* and has done countless radio shows.

Dr. Block welcomes hearing from readers. He can be contacted at *drblock@drblock.com* or through his website, *www.drblock.com.*

Photo courtesy of John Ganun.

Kimberly Dawn Neumann is a popular New York City–based writer who frequently covers the dating/relationship/sex beat. A Summa cum Laude graduate of the University of Maryland School of Journalism (first in her class), her advice articles have appeared in such magazines as *Cosmopolitan*, *Redbook*, *Marie Claire*, *Maxim*, *Health*, and regularly online for the sites at MSN, AOL, and Match.com. As a dating expert and host, she has given online dating and relationship advice to TV/radio audiences from Las Vegas to Chicago to Australia. Consulting for Match.com, she has written online dating guides, given profile pointers, and found herself a date or two along the way. In collaboration with psychologist Joel D. Block, PhD, she proudly debuted her first book, *The Real Reasons Men Commit: Why He Will—or Won't—Love, Honor and Marry You* (Adams Media) in 2008 and was thrilled to follow up that adventure with *Sex Comes First*. A seasoned Broadway performer in addition to being a writer, she has appeared onstage in many classic shows including *Ragtime*, *A Chorus Line*, and *Annie Get Your Gun*. She thinks relationships are fascinating and loves her work in this genre. For more, visit *www.KDNeumann.com*.

INDEX

Index

Trust
lies and, 22–26
little things that damage, 21–23
loss of, 23–26
love and, 19–21
repairing, 27–31
sex and, 26–27
sexual solution to repairing,
31–34
Twenty questions, 61–62
Unrecognized anger, 4–5
Unresolved anger, 5–6
Unvoiced anger, 3–4

Vacations, 125
Volume, 89

Webcams, 129–30
Weekends, 124
Women, expressions of affection
by, 188–89
Work
bringing home, 121
conversations about, 122
relationships and, 115–18,
120–25
sex and, 118–20
sexual solution to too much,
125–30
Work travel, 119

Yin/Yang game, 80–83
Yin/Yang polarity
communication and, 70–73
gender resynchronization and,
75–79
sex and, 73–74